What Mummy Makes

REBECCA WILSON

Cook just once for you
and your baby

For Nina

This book is for you, my Nini,
watching you enjoy mama's cooking
brings me such joy and immense pride.
I love you darling.

Contents

BLUEBERRY PANCAKE BITES, SEE PAGE 41

Hello, Rebecca here!

This book is all about family food. Meals that the whole family can sit and eat together. From 6-month-olds just starting on their culinary adventure and fussy toddlers experimenting with food refusal, to time-pressed mums, dads and grandparents who love nothing more than to spend time with their family; everyone can sit around the table and enjoy every recipe in this book, together!

When I was a little girl, I would help my mum to cook our family meals, then we would all sit around the dining table and eat together as a family, discussing the ingredients and talking about our day. I'm a big believer that this is the reason why I enjoy food so much now! Studies show that eating with your child, modelling and enjoying mealtimes together are really important. Firstly, it helps baby and toddler learn how to eat by watching the people around them enjoy the same food, but secondly, it combats fussiness by having happy, healthy mealtime role models. Eating together as a family instils a healthy eating routine so mealtimes become less of a struggle. Most importantly, it means we only need to cook once!

In this book, I guide you through the most commonly asked questions when first starting to wean a baby onto solid food. But most importantly, I invite you to cook the easy and delicious family meals that I share with my daughter. I hope to give you the confidence to feed your family and enjoy eating together.

MY WEANING JOURNEY

When Nina started to wean onto solid foods, I felt like a rabbit in the headlights. Purées or finger foods? Do I need to start with baby rice? What textures are safe for baby? What can, and can't, I serve to her? So many questions, and with so many sources of information, I wasn't sure who to trust.

I personally began Nina's weaning journey with purées alongside a mixture of finger foods. Focusing on sharing meals with Nina, I offered her a puréed version of my meal, along with a small selection of the food in finger strip form, so she was able to explore different textures from the same taste. After a month or so had passed, Nina started to refuse the spoon so we went for a pure baby-led weaning method.

It's important to note that this is mine and Nina's weaning journey, and it may look completely different to yours. This is totally fine – every baby is different, and every baby will eat differently.

YOUR WEANING JOURNEY

Every recipe in this book has been created with time-pressed parents in mind and as such every single one can be cooked in under 30 minutes – check the timings next to the stopwatch symbol (⏱). All the prep is as simple as it can be, so you can get it done in between changing nappies and helping with homework.

I know that weaning your little one can be worrying so I've labelled each recipe so you can tell what's suitable for your family at a glance. All the recipes are safe to serve right from the start of your journey. Look out for these symbols:

⭐	#WMMclassic	V	Vegetarian
GF	Gluten free	Vg	Vegan
EF	Egg free	DF	Dairy free

Whenever you see a * next to the letters in the symbols, this indicates that recipes can be adapted to suit this dietary requirement. Please take care and look for the substitutions listed in the ingredients. This is especially important for parents looking to introduce cow's milk and other milk products like oat or soya (soy) milk – see page 207 for more information.

No salt has been used in any of these recipes to accommodate for the little ones. If you are a salt fiend, season your portion at the table.

Rebecca Wilson

A note about nutrition

As a Paediatric Dietitian and Feeding Therapist, I have supported families with their children's diets and feeding for my entire career. In this time, I have often reflected that feeding children is an aspect of parenting that can bring equal measures of unease, frustration or anxiety coupled with delight, reward and at times complete elation! Equally, for children, what and how they are fed can have a significant impact on their health and happiness, both during childhood but extending throughout their life.

When you discuss why food and eating are so important with children, families and healthcare professionals alike, the answer almost instinctively relates to two features that are unique to feeding but can be summarized as nourishment. From a nutrition perspective this acknowledges the necessity of food for life, growth, development and good health. Holistically it also encompasses the importance of nurturing elements such as; skill development, learning opportunities, socialization, experience, celebration, nostalgia and love.

The importance of nutrition for babies and children is unquestionable. They have unique requirements for energy and nutrients to support rapid growth, physical and brain development. Alongside this, feeding and eating habits from birth onwards lay foundations for later health and prevention of disease. With this in mind, there are times where paying some extra attention to eating, both from a nutrition and behavioural perspective, will be a well-returned investment. One of these stages is from the introduction of complementary feeding (weaning) onwards into the early preschool years. In fact, the first 1,000 days (from pregnancy to a child's 2nd birthday) are well acknowledged to be a critical window to optimize nutrition, growth and feeding behaviours. Unsurprisingly, this is also a time where parents often describe feeling a huge amount of pressure about "getting it right", worrying about their child "getting enough" or when common nutritional challenges such as food allergy or fussy eating add additional layers of concern or catering conundrums. Within all our different cultures, feeding children is an area that also appears to come with a side dish of what I like to term "nutrition noise", opinion or myths, which can make the whole process feel like a complete minefield.

What is important to remember is that getting a few simple but key practices in place can be enough to allow you and your child to feel relaxed, empowered and reap the nourishing benefits of mealtimes together. Weaved throughout Rebecca's book between her creative and delicious family meals, is not just her infectious, pragmatic and positive outlook on feeding children, but a "recipe" of evidence-based "ingredients" to support your child's eating including;

For this recipe you will need...

- Nutritious meals and snacks that are not only easy to make but also deliver essential nutrients for growth, development and health.

- Variety both with the range of foods to provide nutritional diversity, and also the way they are presented and offered. Variety really is key when feeding children, as each different texture, shape, colour and presentation of a food helps to support your child's acceptance and tolerance of change long term, whilst embedding key feeding skills and experience.

- Family meals with recipes that are designed to be one meal eaten together! We know that family mealtimes are an essential ingredient for supporting children's feeding habits and managing fussy eating. Sharing mealtimes allows endless and repeated opportunity for benefits such as role modelling, exposure, experience and expansion with food.

- Balance, both from a perspective of nourishment with nutrition but also with a view that food should be enjoyed without earning potential, negative connotations, or pressure to be consumed.

- Inclusivity by identifying recipes suitable for key dietary needs and allergen avoidance, meaning everyone can continue to enjoy safe but tasty and nutritious meals together. This can have huge benefits for children with medical nutrition needs such as food allergy, who so often are identified as having lower quality of life scores, including around feeding.

- Rich sensory experiences with the use of different preparation methods, foods and encouraging children to use all of their senses with eating, including getting messy!

- Protected time for mealtimes, away from distractions and the stresses of the day to focus on those other nurturing moments such as talking, laughing, sharing, socializing and learning.

- Reduced pressure on both yourself and your child. Eating can be an emotive subject, but by keeping anxiety and expectation away from food and mealtimes you're more likely to support not hinder the process.

So, sit down, grab a cuppa and enjoy making mealtimes, good times!

Lucy Upton
Specialist Paediatric Dietitian & Feeding Therapist
The Feeding Trust

WHEN SHOULD I START TO WEAN MY BABY?

Introducing your baby to solid foods should begin when they are about 6 months of age and showing all the developmental signs of readiness:

- Baby will be able to stay in the sitting position and hold their head steadily for at least 60 seconds. Ensure baby is not leaning on you or another object, they need to be able to sit up straight independently.
- Your baby will be able to coordinate their eyes, hands and mouth so they can look at food, pick it up and then bring the food to their mouth.
- Baby will be able to swallow food, rather than spit it out. If you start offering solid food and baby spits it all out, wait a couple of days and try again.

Often other behavioural traits are mistaken for signs of readiness, such as:

- Waking more in the night, or not yet sleeping through.
- Chewing on fists – this is often teething or a developmental mannerism.
- Wanting extra milk feeds – offer extra milk if you feel your baby wants this.

When you feel it's the right time to start offering your baby solid foods, choose a time of day when your baby is relaxed and happy. Not too tired and not too hungry, but equally not too full from their last milk feed. Always offer baby solid food first and then follow up with breast or formula milk after the meal if you feel baby wants a little top up. There is no right or wrong here, the idea is to ensure baby is hungry enough to try new foods, but in the beginning they won't be eating enough solids to fill them up.

For more information on how your baby's milk feeds will change during weaning turn to page 207.

SO LET'S WEIGH UP THE OPTIONS...

How you wean your baby is really up to you, and what fits in with your family dynamic. Whether you do the traditional purée method or go down the baby-led weaning route, there is no right or wrong. And it's very important to note that you can 100 per cent do both, and by doing so you will get the best of both worlds. The aim in weaning baby onto solid foods is to teach them how to process food in their mouth efficiently, raise a confident eater who is used to eating a wide variety of flavours, and to enjoy family mealtimes together. The most important thing is to ensure baby is exposed to a wide variety of tastes and textures, and to offer them well-balanced and nutrient-rich foods.

WHY OFFER FINGER FOODS?

Letting baby explore food in its whole state allows them to familiarize themselves more quickly with this new concept of eating, as well as develop their hand-eye coordination and fine motor skills. Studies also show that allowing baby to learn to chew early on helps to develop their speech.

By letting baby take control of their eating in this way, they will learn how to chew and swallow more efficiently, which can, in turn, make the weaning process less stressful. It also helps support their natural ability to self regulate, to understand hunger and fullness, and gain independence.

Finger foods make family eating much easier. You can all enjoy a wide variety of family meals together, introducing baby to many tastes and textures. This can make them less fussy as they grow older. Rest assured, there is no more risk of baby choking when feeding baby finger foods as opposed to purées.

WHY PURÉE?

Offering baby purées is an easy way to introduce solid foods to baby, in a way that is more manageable and familiar for your little one. It's important to note that if you decide to offer baby puréed food, be mindful that you should introduce thicker and lumpier textures within a couple of days of starting to wean baby. Once you feel comfortable, introduce finger foods alongside purées. You can start with steamed vegetables, then move on to other flavours, by offering baby finger food from the recipes in this book.

WHAT SHOULD BABY'S FIRST TASTES BE?

It is recommended for baby's very first tastes to be single vegetables (bitter green ones are preferable) in the form of vegetable purée or fingers. It's important to offer a wide variety of tastes from day one. By starting with vegetables, baby gets used to these new tastes and textures. Breast and formula milk is quite sweet, which most babies naturally prefer the taste of, so by introducing new bitter flavours from day one of weaning, it ensures that baby doesn't gain a preference for sweet things.

TO OFFER AS A PURÉE

Mash the veg with the back of a fork or blend in a blender with a little of baby's usual milk to help loosen the consistency. It is fine to completely blitz the veg to a smooth purée, but aim to progress to thicker and more textured foods as soon as possible, so that baby doesn't become accustomed to a certain consistency. Variety is key.

TO OFFER AS A FINGER FOOD

Ensure the veg is cut into finger strips, around 7.5cm (3in) long and 1cm (½in) wide. This is just so it is easy for baby to hold, so no need to get the ruler out!

Soft steam or boil vegetable strips or batons, around the length of your finger. For the first 2 weeks, cook them for longer than you would usually; around 10-12 minutes. You want the veg to mash easily when pressed between your thumb and forefinger.

For the best of both worlds, offer both purée and finger food of the same food.

After a week or two of just offering a variety of veg, if you feel baby is ready to move on, you can start to make all the recipes in this book.

Do not worry if your baby doesn't actually eat much for a while or you can't figure out how much baby has actually swallowed. At this stage it's not about filling their tummies up with food – there is milk for that. Right now, it's all about exposing baby to a variety of tastes and textures.

MY TOP TIPS TO ENCOURAGE BABY TO EAT
- Lots of praise and encouragement, smiling and talking to baby as they eat.
- Always eat the same food as baby. They learn how to eat from watching you.
- Make mealtimes fun so they look forward to going in the highchair. Get some happy music on and, as much as possible, involve the whole family.
- Try to set a consistent routine, so baby gets to know what happens when they go into the highchair. Ensure the telly is off and there are no distracting toys in eye-sight.
- Go at baby's pace and don't rush mealtimes. Baby will tell you when they have had enough food or if they would like more.
- It can take up to 10 or more tries of offering a new food to baby before they accept it, so don't be discouraged if they refuse something. Keep offering it regularly and sooner or later baby will give it a go.

When will my baby be ready to move to more than one meal a day?
Initially offer baby only one meal a day, so the transition to eating solid food isn't too much. Once you feel like a small routine is forming and you are happy with how weaning is going, you can now think about introducing a second meal. And again with adding a third meal. With my Nina, she was on two meals by 7 months and eating three meals a day by 8 months.

Try not to worry about "normal" meal times or compare to when other babies eat. Every baby's schedule is different, it will all work itself out as time passes.

Weaning your baby is such an exciting time, but it's normal to feel daunted. Try and trust your gut, you've got this!

FREEZER STASH!
If you decide to make purées for baby, make life easy and blend enough to freeze portions in an ice-cube tray. You can take 1-2 cubes out to defrost at a time and puréed vegetables will keep frozen for up to 3 months. These are also great to add to stews and pasta sauces for an extra dose of veggies.

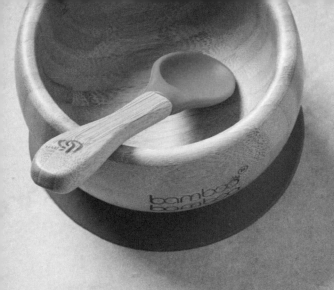

WEANING EQUIPMENT CHECKLIST

You don't need much when weaning baby, but there are a few must haves.

- A **highchair** with a **safety harness.** Never leave baby unattended when they are eating. If your highchair has shoulder straps, ensure they aren't so tight that baby is leaning back, and cannot bring themselves forward. If baby was to gag on a piece of food, we want them to be able to lean forward to dislodge the item themselves.
- A **small cup**, such as an open cup or valve-free sippy cup. It's good to get your baby used to drinking water from an open cup as soon as possible. Until 12 months old, babies don't need additional hydration, their breast or formula milk will be enough, this is mostly just for practice.
- Use **soft weaning utensils** at first, which are kinder on baby's gums than metal spoons. And as you progress with weaning you can let baby use a **soft grip toddler spoon and fork** to help them try and feed themselves using cutlery.
- A good **catcher or long-sleeve bib.**
- **Small bamboo or silicone bowl and plate**, preferably with good suction.
- **Storage boxes** for the fridge and freezer.

A DAY IN THE LIFE OF A WEANING BABY

Please note this is just an example feeding schedule. As time goes by the timings and feeds will change. Every baby has different milk feeds, and breastfed babies in particular can change their daily routine very frequently. Not all babies need additional snacks, see page 202.

6 MONTHS

7am	milk
10am	milk
11am	solids
12:30pm	milk
4pm	milk
7pm	milk

(Plus your baby's usual milk feeds during the night.)

7 MONTHS

7am	milk
7:30am	solids
10am	milk
12pm	milk
1pm	solids
4pm	milk
7pm	milk

(Plus your baby's usual milk feeds during the night.)

8–9 MONTHS

7am	milk
8am	breakfast
10:30am	snack
12:30pm	lunch
3pm	milk
5.30pm	dinner
7pm	milk

(Plus your baby's usual milk feeds during the night.)

10–12 MONTHS

7am	wake
7:30am	breakfast
10am	snack
12:30pm	lunch
3pm	snack
5.30pm	dinner
7pm	milk

(Plus your baby's usual milk feeds during the night.)

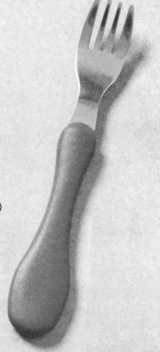

FOODS TO AVOID WHEN WEANING BABY

You can serve most food to baby, but there are some foods that aren't suitable for little tummies:

SALT

Babies and children shouldn't eat too much salt as it isn't good for their kidneys. Therefore avoid adding salt to baby's meals, which also includes salt in pasta or vegetable cooking water. All the recipes in this book have no salt added to them. Adults, you may want to season your portion at the dinner table.

Babies under 12 months should have less than 1g of salt per day (0.4g of sodium).
Toddlers aged 1–3 years can have a maximum of 2g of salt (0.8g of sodium).
Children aged 4–6 years are allowed 3g of salt per day (1.2g of sodium).
Children aged 7–10 years can have a maximum of 5g of salt per day
(2g of sodium).
Children aged 11 years to adulthood can have a maximum of 6g of salt per day (2.4g of sodium).

To put that into relative terms, a slice of shop-bought medium sliced white bread contains on average 0.4g of salt. So when you're feeding baby, keep a little rough calculation in your head of what they have eaten that day. Do note though, you may serve 1 slice of toast to baby, but they may not eat all of it.

Remember that these figures are just guidelines. It's good practice to look at baby's intake across the whole week rather than just one meal.

SUGAR

Try to avoid too many sugary treats for little ones, as over-exposure to sweet tastes can lead to a preference for sugary flavours. This also includes naturally occurring sugars in foods like fresh fruit juices, as this can lead to tooth decay.

SATURATED FAT

Babies and young children need lots of fat in their diet as they are using lots of energy growing, learning and being active, so choose full-fat versions of dairy products like milk or cheese. However, do be mindful to limit your child's intake of saturated fat in foods like cakes, biscuits (cookies) and crisps (chips).

WHOLE NUTS

Avoid serving whole nuts and peanuts to babies and children under the age of 5 years as they are a choking hazard.

Nut butters, crushed and ground nuts can be served to baby from around the age of 6 months. See page 208 for advice on how to introduce this allergen into baby's diet.

RAW EGGS

From 6 months you can serve eggs to baby. In the UK, choose hen's eggs that have the British Lion quality stamp on them, which are safe to serve raw as an ingredient in food like homemade mayonnaise, or lightly cooked like a soft-boiled egg.

If the eggs are not British Lion stamped or you are in doubt, always fully cook the white and yolk of the egg until they are solid before serving to baby. This also includes duck, goose or quail's eggs.

HONEY

Honey can contain bacteria that can produce toxins in baby's intestines leading to infant botulism, which is a very serious illness. Avoid serving honey to babies under the age of 12 months. This includes shop-bought products that contain honey in the ingredients, so always read the packaging.

CERTAIN CHEESES

Cheese is packed full of calcium, protein and vitamins, making it a fantastic food to serve to babies and young children as part of a varied diet. However, it is advised to offer only pasteurized full-fat cheese from the age of 6 months. This includes hard cheese, like Cheddar, cottage cheese and soft cream cheese.

There is a risk of the bacteria listeria in soft cheese like brie, camembert, ripened goat's cheese, blue cheese or cheese made from unpasteurized milk. Listeria can make baby feel very ill so it's best to avoid. However, you can use these cheeses to cook with, as the listeria is killed when cooking.

RICE DRINKS

Babies and young children up to the age of 5 years, shouldn't drink rice-based drinks, especially not as a replacement for breast or formula milk, as it contains high levels of arsenic. Babies are fine to eat rice as the levels are monitored in the EU for rice and rice-based products.

RAW SHELLFISH

Always fully cook shellfish such as mussels, oysters, clams and cockles to avoid the risk of food poisoning.

SHARK, SWORDFISH AND MARLIN

Avoid shark, swordfish or marlin as the high levels of mercury found in them can affect the development of baby's nervous system.

HOW TO CUT AND SERVE FOOD FOR BABY

So we know that eating the same food as baby is really important, however, practically how do you do it?

The trick is to cut all food, where possible, into finger strips, about 7.5cm (3in) long and 1cm (½in) wide. You want the food to be long enough so baby can hold it in their fist with half the length sticking out the top of their hand to nibble on. Use your forefinger as a general guide.

A FEW EXAMPLES:
- **Toast** – cut into strips.
- **Hard-boiled egg** – cut into quarters, lengthways.
- **Avocado** – cut into wedges (for younger babies, leave some of the skin still attached to aid with grip).
- **Kiwi** – peel and cut into rounds or wedges lengthways.
- **Cooked chicken** – removed from the bone and cut into strips.
- **Fritters/pancakes** – cut into strips.
- **Grapes** – cut into quarters lengthways.
- **Blueberries** – squish or cut in half.
- **Nuts** – never serve whole nuts to children under 5; always finely crush or serve in nut butter form.
- **Corn on the cob** – cut into 2.5cm (1in) rounds once cooked.
- **Nectarine** – cut in half, remove the stone (pit) and cut each half into wedges.
- **Peas and sweetcorn** – these are too small to be a choking hazard, so can be served whole.

FOODS THAT NEED A SPOON
Yogurt, for example, can be spoon-fed to baby, or have two spoons on the go and preload one for baby to pick up and feed themselves. You can also add fruit strips dunked into it. You can serve food like hummus with lots of different dippers stuck into it to encourage baby to learn how to dunk. Or try serving thick soup with bread fingers dunked into it.

ARE YOU WORRIED ABOUT CHOKING?

It's such a big concern and something that should be taken seriously when feeding your child. However, it's really important to not let the fear of choking hold you back from serving a variety of foods to your baby. There is no greater risk of choking when serving finger foods vs purées to baby. It's a good idea to attend a first aid course or research baby CPR online, so you have the knowledge behind you if the worst happens.

When your baby first starts to eat, they will gag a little, some babies more than others. This is completely normal. Babies have a natural strong gag reflex, which is designed to stop them choking on their tongue when lying down.

GAGGING VS CHOKING

It can be really hard, but try not to panic when your baby gags. Although it may seem the same, it's very different to choking. Gagging is baby's reflex reaction to move food forward from the back of the mouth. Choking is when an object is lodged in baby's throat and blocking their airways.

A general rule is to listen for sound. If baby is coughing or making grunting noises and can still visibly breathe, then this is gagging, and extremely normal. Your little one's face may go a little red, but likely it won't be harmful for baby and they will carry on eating. If baby is choking, there will be no sound, and baby's chest will be pulled in as they struggle to breathe.

Although gagging can be difficult to witness with your little baby, it's important for them to learn how to deal with food in their mouth and this is their way of learning. If you panic or try to remove the food from baby's mouth when they are gagging, this can in turn lead to baby choking on the food item. (However, if baby is making no noise and is visibly choking on the item, don't hesitate to step in and help baby dislodge the food from their airway, by quickly removing baby from the highchair, patting them on the back with baby leaning forward, and following the baby CPR process.)

There are certain steps you can take to avoid your baby choking when feeding:

- Ensure baby is developmentally ready to start eating solid food
- Ensure they can sit up straight, unaided for at least 60 seconds.
- Ensure baby is able to coordinate their hands and eyes, to be able to pick up food and bring it to their mouth.
- If serving finger food to baby, always let baby hold the food to their mouth themselves, do not hold the food in baby's mouth.
- Ensure baby is sitting in an appropriate highchair, their back is straight and they are sitting upright.
- Don't serve food to baby in walkers or bouncers. Sudden movements can be dangerous.
- Cut and serve food appropriately, and avoid hard foods like raw carrot.
- Never leave baby unattended while they are eating.
- Avoid too many distractions so your baby can concentrate on eating.
- Always model how to eat the food you are serving to your baby.

Breakfast

BABY PORRIDGE FINGERS

This is a simple method for serving nutritious porridge to babies in a way they can feed themselves! You can replace the cow's milk with a dairy-free alternative and add berries, nut butters or grated apple for flavour.

GF

EF

V

Vg*

DF*

🍴 1 adult and 1 little
⏱ 5 minutes

about 12 tbsp rolled
  (old-fashioned)
  porridge oats
about 12 tbsp milk of
  your choice*
pinch of ground
  cinnamon (optional)
about 12 x 12cm (5 x 5in)
  microwaveable
  container

Half-fill a container with porridge oats, counting the number of spoonfuls it takes. (I used 12 tbsp oats for my container, but you may need more or less if your container is a different size.)

Add the same amount of milk as you did oats, so you have a 50:50 mix of oats to milk. Add the cinnamon, if using, stir and flatten the mixture with the back of the spoon. Little ones can help with putting the oats, milk and cinnamon into the tub.

Microwave on high for 2 minutes. If the mixture feels firm, it's ready; if it's still quite soft, cook for a further minute or so. It will continue to firm up as it cools. Allow to stand for a couple of minutes, then cut it into finger strips using a knife, turn out onto a board to cool. Serve with full-fat Greek-style yogurt and berries.

Store in the fridge for a couple of days, or freeze for 3 months.

COURGETTE EGGY FINGERS

A really great way to serve egg to babies from 6 months, with all the major food groups in one dish – protein, veg, carbs and healthy fats. Just 5 minutes prep, too!

GF

V

🍴 10 fingers
⏱ 30 minutes

1 small courgette (zucchini)
60g (2oz) Cheddar
6 eggs
2 tbsp rolled (old-
  fashioned) porridge oats
black pepper
900g (2lb) non-stick loaf
  tin, greased with olive
  or coconut oil cooking
  spray

Preheat the oven to 180°C fan (200°C/400°F/Gas 6).

Coarsely grate the courgette and cheese into a bowl. Crack in the eggs, add the oats and a pinch of black pepper. Using a fork, whisk together until combined.

Pour the mixture into the greased tin, and bake for about 20–25 minutes, until the middle feels set when pressed slightly. Allow to cool for 5 minutes before tipping out onto a board and cutting into fingers 2cm (¾in) wide.

Store in the fridge for 2 days or in the freezer for 3 months.

EGGY BREAD TWO WAYS

Eggy bread is such a great finger food option – and can be prepped and cooked in under 10 minutes. It is full of nutrients, super soft and easy for babies to eat from 6 months – simply cut them into fingers.

RASPBERRY AND BANANA EGGY BREAD

🍴 4 slices
⏱ 10 minutes

1 small snack-sized
    banana, or ½ regular
    banana
about 15 raspberries
2 eggs
1 tsp pure vanilla extract
4 slices white bread
sunflower oil, unsalted
    butter or olive oil, for
    frying

Mash the banana with the back of a fork. A few lumps are totally fine. Add the raspberries and mash again. Little hands can help with this bit; you may just need to help them get the lumps out. Add the eggs and vanilla extract and whisk until combined.

Place a large non-stick frying pan over a medium heat with a little drizzle of your choice of fat for frying.

Dip a piece of bread in the egg mixture, ensuring there's no dry bread visible, and add to the pan. In batches of two, fry each piece of bread for 2 minutes on each side until all the egg has cooked, and the eggy bread has taken on a scrumptious golden colour. Turn down the heat if the bread is colouring too quickly.

Cut into fingers and serve with some extra raspberries.

SPINACH AND CHEESE EGGY BREAD

🍴 4 slices
⏱ 10 minutes

60g (2oz) frozen
    chopped spinach
    (about 3 blocks)
35g (1oz) Cheddar, grated
3 eggs
4 slices white bread
sunflower or olive oil,
    for frying

Microwave the spinach for 2 minutes or until defrosted. Using a fork, gently press the spinach to remove the excess moisture. Add the spinach to a high-sided plate with the grated cheese and eggs. Whisk with a fork until everything is incorporated.

Place a large non-stick frying pan over a medium heat with a little drizzle of oil for frying.

Dip a piece of bread in the egg mixture, making sure you have plenty of spinach and cheese on each side of the bread (you can use a spoon for this, but I find fingers work best). Add to the pan.

In batches of two, fry each piece of bread for 2 minutes on each side until deliciously golden and crispy. Cut into fingers and serve with full-fat Greek-style yogurt for dipping, if you like.

MEXICAN BAKED EGGS

Inspired by the classic Mexican breakfast, Huevos Rancheros is a dish traditionally made up of black beans, tomato salsa, tortillas and fried eggs. This one-pan baked version makes it super easy to bring some Latino vibes to your Sunday brunching!

🍴 4 adults and 4 littles
⏱ 20 minutes

1 tbsp tomato purée (paste)
1 tsp dried basil
1 tsp dried oregano
juice of 1 lime
1 tsp smoked paprika
1 tsp garlic granules
pinch of ground cumin
400g can good-quality chopped tomatoes
2 x 230g cans black beans in water, drained and rinsed (ensure no added salt)
4 large tortilla wraps
150g (5½oz) Cheddar, grated
150ml (5½fl oz) sour cream, plus extra to serve
6 eggs
freshly ground black pepper
1 large avocado, sliced, to serve

Preheat the oven to 200°C fan (220°C/425°F/Gas 7).

In a medium bowl, mix together the tomato purée and 100ml (3½fl oz) cold water to a runny paste, then add the basil, oregano, lime juice, smoked paprika, garlic granules, cumin, a good grinding of black pepper and the canned tomatoes. Mix well.

Take a large ovenproof dish, big enough for a tortilla to fit in (if the tortilla folds up a little on the sides, it's okay). Add the rinsed black beans to the dish. Use a potato masher to mash the beans into a purée. Spoon the bean paste into a bowl and set aside.

Take 2 tbsp of the tomato mixture and spread it thinly across the base of the dish. Place 2 tortilla wraps in the dish, to cover the tomato sauce. Spoon over the black bean paste, and spread out evenly using the back of a spoon. Cover the bean paste with half of the remaining tomato sauce and distribute it evenly across the dish. Sprinkle over 100g (3½oz) of the grated cheese, then top with the remaining 2 tortilla wraps.

Dollop the remaining tomato sauce sporadically across the top of the dish. Then do the same with the sour cream, adding it where there is no tomato sauce. Using your spoon, gently and really briefly ripple the sour cream into the tomato sauce and rustically cover the surface of the dish. With the back of the spoon, make 6 wells in the sauce for the eggs to sit in. Space them well apart.

Crack an egg into each well, trying to keep the yolks intact. Sprinkle the remaining cheese over the dish, making sure not to cover the egg yolks with the cheese. Finish with an extra grinding of black pepper, then pop in the oven for 15 minutes, or until the egg white has set. If your eggs are not British lion-stamped, cook for a further 5 minutes to completely set the egg yolk, too.

Serve with more sour cream on the side and slices of avocado.

This will need chopping up for your little ones, which doesn't look super pretty, but it'll make it easier for them to eat. Everything is soft, so suitable for babies to pick up pieces and nibble on.

MAKE IT MINI!
You can halve the quantities and make this recipe in a smaller dish. Cut the tortillas in half so you can layer it up to fit in your desired dish.

SCRAMBLED EGGS TWO WAYS

Eggs are a fantastic source of protein and healthy fats, as well as packed full of vital vitamins and nutrients. Upgrade the humble scrambled egg with these combos!

COTTAGE CHEESE AND CHIVE SCRAMBLED EGGS

🍴 **2 adults and 2 littles**
⏱ **5 minutes**

small knob (pat) of
    unsalted butter
4 eggs
2 heaped tbsp cottage
    cheese
1 tbsp chopped chives
freshly ground black
    pepper

Place a large, heavy-bottomed, non-stick frying pan over a medium heat, add the butter and let it melt.

Meanwhile whisk together the eggs, cottage cheese, two-thirds of the chives and a good grinding of black pepper in a bowl.

Once the butter has melted, add the egg mixture to the pan. Using a rubber spatula, keep moving the eggs around the pan quickly and constantly, ensuring to keep scraping the mixture off from the base of the pan.

Stirring constantly, cook for 2–3 minutes, or until all the egg has cooked and firmed up, and most of the moisture has evaporated.

Serve on toast, crumpets or pikelets, sprinkled with the remaining chopped chives.

SPINACH AND CHEESE SCRAMBLED EGGS

🍴 **2 adults and 2 littles**
⏱ **5 minutes**

small knob (pat) of
    unsalted butter
large handful of baby leaf
    spinach
4 eggs
40g (1½oz) Cheddar,
    grated
freshly ground black
    pepper

Place a large, heavy-bottomed, non-stick frying pan over a medium heat, add the butter and let it melt.

Meanwhile, roughly chop the spinach using a large knife, then add to the frying pan. Stir and cook until the spinach has wilted.

Meanwhile whisk the eggs, cheese and a good grinding of black pepper together in a bowl. Once the spinach has wilted and you see no more water in the pan, add the eggs.

Using a rubber spatula, keep moving the eggs around the pan ensuring to keep scraping the mixture off from the base of the pan to eliminate the risk of an unwanted flaky texture.

Once the eggs are cooked all the way through, and are light and bouncy, transfer to a plate and serve with buttered toast fingers. Or try serving wrapped in a quick homemade yogurt flatbread (see page 44) for an alternative to toasted bread products.

SMOKEY BEANS ON TOAST

GF*

EF

V*

Vg*

DF*

With no salt or sugar (which the usual shop-bought varieties are packed with), these delicious beans are perfect for the whole family to enjoy. Toast is one of those simple go-to breakfasts that I steer towards on busy mornings. When shopping for bread, or crumpets or English muffins, try to choose a variety with the lowest amount of salt. If baby eats two-thirds of a piece of toast, do a little calculation in your head to ensure the amount of salt per slice isn't too high. Aim for roughly 0.3–0.4g of salt per serving. Don't worry if it's a little higher, as salt intake should be viewed over the course of a week rather than each specific meal. Serve toast in finger strips for baby so its easier for them to pick up.

🍴 2 adults and 2 littles
⏱ 10 minutes

2 x 400g cans haricot
(navy) beans in water
(ensure no added salt)
2 tbsp tomato purée
(paste)
2 tsp smoked paprika
½ tsp mixed dried herbs
1 tsp Worcestershire
sauce (optional*)
freshly ground black
pepper

Add all the ingredients to a saucepan, including the bean water, with a good grinding of black pepper. Stir and let it simmer for 8–10 minutes until the beans have softened and the sauce has thickened. Haricot beans are too small to be a choking hazard, however you can mash the beans into the sauce a little to serve to baby if you desire.

Serve on buttered toast (check for gluten- and dairy free, if required*) with an optional (or essential in some households!) grating of cheese on top.

These beans will keep in the fridge for up to 3 days or in the freezer for 3 months. Defrost and reheat in the pan with an extra splash of water to help loosen the consistency. Ensure all reheated food is piping hot before cooling and serving.

OTHER FAMILY-FRIENDLY TOAST TOPPING OPTIONS

- mashed avocado
- full-fat cream cheese
- unsalted butter
- 100% peanut or almond butter
- sugar-free jam, see page 192
- super-ripe or soft fruits, such as plums and berries, which can be mashed with a fork
- tahini (sesame seed paste) with fresh berries
- cottage cheese
- hummus, see page 45
- mashed banana sprinkled with cinnamon
- pesto, see page 64
- scrambled or mashed hard-boiled eggs

BABY-FRIENDLY GRANOLA

Whip up a batch of this low-sugar granola in just 30 minutes and it'll store for 2 weeks ready for quick, healthy breakfasts. Pulse to a fine crumb for babies from 6 months of age or to a crunchy texture for toddlers. From the age of 3, you can serve this granola as it comes, without breaking it down.

GF
EF
V
Vg*
DF*

🍴 3 adults and 6 littles
⏱ 20 minutes

80g (3oz) shop-bought 100% apple purée (use a baby food pouch) or mashed banana (about 1 medium banana)
2 tbsp coconut oil, melted
1 tsp pure vanilla extract
2 tbsp honey or maple syrup* (optional, honey should only be served to babies over 12 months)
250g (9oz) rolled (old-fashioned) porridge oats
4 tbsp poppy seeds
100g (3½oz) flaked (sliced) almonds
40g (1½oz) pumpkin seeds
40g (1½oz) sunflower seeds
60g (2oz) walnuts, roughly crushed
100g (3½oz) (dark) seedless raisins
40g (1½oz) unsweetened flaked coconut
large baking tray, lined with non-stick baking paper

Preheat the oven to 200°C fan (220°C/425°F/Gas 7).

In a large bowl, mix together the fruit purée, melted coconut oil, vanilla extract and honey or maple syrup.

Stir in the oats, seeds and crushed nuts until everything has been coated a little in the liquid. Spread over the baking tray in a thin and even layer. Bake in the preheated oven for 7 minutes.

After 7 minutes, add the raisins and coconut, stir well using two spatulas and spread back out into an even layer. If there are any nuts that have started to colour quickly, hide them down inside the granola layer, so they don't burn. Pop the tray back in the oven for 5 minutes more. Check again, stir, then pop back in the oven for 2–4 minutes, making sure the nuts aren't burning, as they will catch easily towards the end of the cooking.

Allow to cool. Store in an airtight container in a cool dark place for up to 2 weeks.

NOTES ABOUT NUTS

Whole nuts are a choking hazard before the age of 5, which is why flaked and crushed nuts have been used in this recipe. You can use whole nuts to make this granola too, just ensure you blitz or crush with a rolling pin before serving to younger children.

To make this granola suitable for children under the age of 3, spoon half (or as much as you wish) of the granola into a food processor and blitz on full power for a couple of minutes until the nuts, oats and raisins have turned to a powder. If your child is toddler age and can handle a little more texture, just briefly pulse the granola until the nuts have broken into smaller pieces.

To serve, stir through yogurt or milk of your choice, and serve with fruit on the side. You can sprinkle the blitzed baby version over porridge or cereals for an extra hit of goodness.

SMOOTHIE BOWLS

The beauty of a smoothie is that you can throw in anything you have, from bananas that are past their best to leafy greens that need using up. Serve smoothies in a bowl with a spoon, or in a sippy or open cup. It may get a little messy, but embrace it! Replace cow's milk or yogurt with plant-based alternatives for dairy-free smoothies.

🍴 **1 adult and 1 little**
⏱ **5 minutes**

BANANA, SPINACH AND BLUEBERRY

1 small banana, fresh or frozen

100g (3½oz) blueberries, fresh or frozen

120ml (4fl oz) milk of your choice*

handful of fresh spinach, or a couple of blocks of frozen spinach

1 tsp ground flaxseeds (linseeds)

PEANUT BUTTER AND JELLY

150g (5½oz) raspberries, fresh or frozen

½ banana, fresh or frozen

1 tbsp smooth 100% peanut butter

100ml (3½fl oz) milk of your choice*

1 tbsp chia seeds

TROPICAL DELIGHT

1 mango, peeled and stoned (pitted), or a handful of frozen mango chunks

juice and pulp of 2 passion fruits (scoop into a sieve (strainer) and press through as much juice using the back of a spoon to remove the seeds)

50g (1¾oz) raspberries, fresh or frozen

100g (3½oz) coconut yogurt

Add all the ingredients to a blender and whizz until smooth. Store in the fridge for a couple of days, or freeze for up to 3 months.

TOP TIP

Pop your smoothie into a reusable pouch for weaning baby on the go. Or pour into ice lolly moulds for delicious ice pops, which are great for your teething baba!

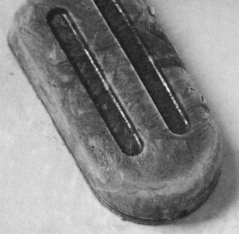

FLAVOURED YOGURT FOUR WAYS

Yogurt is a fantastic source of calcium and protein. The smooth texture means it's a great food to give to baby from 6 months of age. Shop-bought flavoured yogurts often contain high amounts of sugar, so try these combinations to offer baby a wide variety of flavours. However, do be mindful to still offer baby unflavoured or unsweetened yogurts, so they do not generate a sweet preference.

GF

EF

V

Vg*

DF*

🍴 **2 small portions**
⏱ **2 minutes**

BANANA YOGURT
½ banana
3 tbsp thick full-fat Greek-style yogurt, see below*

RASPBERRY YOGURT
10 large raspberries
3 tbsp thick full-fat Greek-style yogurt*

AVOCADO YOGURT
½ large avocado
3 tbsp thick full fat Greek-style yogurt*

SPINACH YOGURT
2 blocks frozen chopped spinach, defrosted
    and excess moisture squeezed out
3 tbsp thick full-fat Greek-style yogurt*

Mash the fruit with the back of a fork and stir in the yogurt. For the spinach combo, simply stir the spinach into the yogurt.

Serve as is on a spoon, spread it on toast, or use it to top porridge, chia pudding or granola.

Left over yogurt can be poured into ice lolly moulds to make ice pops.

MAKE IT VEGAN!
You can substitute cow's milk yogurt for plant-based alternatives, which are available in large supermarkets.

RASPBERRY CHIA PUDDING

Just 2 minutes prep before bed, and the family will wake up to an indulgent but healthy brekkie.

GF

EF

V

Vg*

DF*

🍴 **1 adult and 1 little**
⏱ **2 minutes, plus soaking time**

100g (3½oz) raspberries, fresh or frozen and defrosted
60g (2oz) chia seeds (you can use black or white – white will give a pinker finish)
juice of ¼ lemon
1 tbsp maple syrup or honey* (optional, honey should only be served to babies over 12 months)
200ml (7fl oz) soya (soy) milk (or you can use oat, pea or full-fat cow's milk)*
yogurt of your choice*

Mash the raspberries in a bowl with the back of a fork. Stir in the chia seeds, lemon juice and maple syrup or honey, then add the milk and mix thoroughly.

Cover and place in the fridge overnight or for a minimum of 6 hours.

Serve with a little dollop of full-fat Greek-style yogurt (or dairy-free alternative) and an optional extra drizzle of maple syrup or honey.

This chia pudding will last in the fridge for 3 days, or store in the freezer for up to 2 months.

NUTRITION NOTE
Chia seeds are an excellent source of omega-3 fatty acids, rich in antioxidants and packed full of fibre, iron and calcium.

PIÑA COLADA PORRIDGE

Sweet pineapple lends its comforting flavour to oats here.

🍽 2 adults and 2 littles
⏱ 5 minutes

½ pineapple, or 435g can
   pineapple in juice,
   drained
400ml can coconut milk
rolled (old-fashioned)
   porridge oats
splash of other milk
   of your choice*
1 tbsp desiccated (dried
   unsweetened
   shredded) coconut

Remove the pineapple skin, then grate the pineapple using the coarse side of a box grater, leaving behind the firm middle section. If using canned pineapple, blitz it in a food processor.

Add this to a pan, along with the coconut milk. Fill the empty can with oats up to around three-quarters full. Tip the oats into the pan and give it all a good stir.

Cook on a medium heat for 4 minutes, stirring often until you reach the consistency you desire. You can add a splash of milk to help make the porridge creamier (use a plant-based alternative to cow's milk for dairy-free); cook for another minute to thicken up again. Serve with desiccated coconut on top.

GRAPEFRUIT OVERNIGHT OATS

5 minutes prep before bed and you'll wake up to a healthy breakfast!

🍽 1 adult and 1 little
**⏱ 5 minutes, plus
   soaking time**

juice of 1 grapefruit,
   about 135ml (4½fl oz)
80ml (2½fl oz) milk of
   your choice*
60ml (2fl oz) yogurt
   of your choice*
100g (3½oz) rolled
   (old-fashioned)
   porridge oats
30g (1oz) chia seeds
1 heaped tsp ground
   cinnamon

Squeeze the juice from the grapefruit into a large bowl. Mix in the rest of the ingredients, cover and pop in the fridge overnight.

In the morning, serve straight from the fridge. For a looser consistency, add a splash of cold or warm milk to your bowl.

These overnight oats will last for up to 4 days, stored in the fridge in an airtight container.

SIMPLE SWAPS
Overnight oats are so adaptable. Swap out the grapefruit juice for any other fruit juice, or just more milk. You can add in dried fruits, crushed nuts or grated fruits, such as apple and pear.

BERRY CHEESECAKE BOWL WITH TOASTED OAT CRUMB

This is a brekkie that feels like a delicious treat, but it's full of goodness for you and your little ones to start the day right. It can easily be made dairy-free – see how at the bottom of the page.

🍴 **2 adults and 2 littles**
⏱ **5 minutes**

TOASTED OAT CRUMB
2 tsp unsalted butter*
3 heaped tbsp rolled
  (old-fashioned)
  porridge oats
3 heaped tbsp desiccated
  (dried unsweetened
  shredded) coconut
1 tbsp sesame seeds
1 tbsp maple syrup or
  agave syrup (optional)

CHEESECAKE BOWL
110g (4oz) fresh or frozen
  berries, defrosted if
  frozen
190g (7oz) full-fat cream
  cheese*
180g (6oz) thick full-fat
  Greek-style yogurt*
2 tsp maple syrup, agave
  syrup or honey*
  (optional, honey
  should only be served
  to babies over 12
  months)

Melt the butter in a large non-stick frying pan. Once melted, add the oats, coconut and sesame seeds, and stir together. Cook for a couple of minutes, stirring often so the seeds don't catch. Now add the syrup, if using, stir and cook for a further 2 minutes until it has all turned a lovely golden colour. Once done, take the pan off the heat and set aside while you make the cheesecake bowl.

Add the berries, cream cheese, yogurt and syrup, if using, to a blender and whizz until smooth. Pour into a bowl and sprinkle over the crumb. As the crumb cools, it will stick together a little, so as you sprinkle it over the cheesecake bowl, separate slightly with your fingers. Little ones enjoy helping out with this task!

The crumb will last in an airtight container at room temperature for up to 5 days, and the cheesecake bowl will keep for 3 days in the fridge.

MAKE IT DAIRY-FREE!
- use coconut oil instead of unsalted butter
- use dairy-free cream cheese instead of full-fat cream cheese
- use coconut yogurt instead of full-fat Greek-style yogurt

BACON, CHEESE AND CHIVE MUFFINS

Soft and springy savoury muffins, delicately flavoured with mild chives, moreish bacon and delicious Cheddar cheese. Perfect to fill up the freezer-stash ready for brekkie in a hurry or speedy packed lunches!

EF*

DF*

🍴 **12 muffins**
⏱ **25 minutes**

3 rashers of smoked, thick-cut bacon
drizzle of groundnut oil
3 tbsp finely chopped chives
120g (4oz) Cheddar, grated
220g (8oz) self-raising (self-rising) flour
1 tsp baking powder
4 eggs
70ml (2½fl oz) full-fat (whole) milk
150g (5½oz) unsalted butter, melted
freshly ground black pepper
non-stick 12-hole muffin tin, greased

Preheat the oven to 180°C fan (200°C/400°F/Gas 6).

Cut the bacon in half lengthways, then slice into 1cm (½in) wide pieces. Fry in a frying pan with a teeny drizzle of sunflower oil until crispy.

Add the chopped chives and grated Cheddar to a large mixing bowl with the flour, baking powder, eggs, milk, melted butter, some black pepper and the bacon, along with a little bit of bacon fat from the bottom of the pan. Give it a mix with a spatula until all combined, but try not to over-mix.

Spoon the mixture into the greased muffin tin so that it comes two-thirds of the way up in each section.

Bake in the preheated oven for 15–20 minutes until well risen, golden on top and an inserted knife comes out clean. Transfer to a wire rack to cool before digging in.

Store the muffins in an airtight container at room temperature for 2–3 days, or freeze for up to 3 months.

BLUEBERRY OAT MUFFINS

These delicious oaty muffins, flavoured with cinnamon and bejewelled with juicy blueberries, are the perfect thing to scoff first thing in the morning! Swap the blueberries for raspberries or blackberries, whatever is in season.

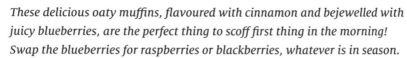

🍴 **12 muffins**

⏱ **30 minutes**

2 ripe bananas

2 eggs or 2 flax eggs, see
   page 140*

90g (3oz) unsalted butter,
   melted or coconut oil
   or dairy free spread*

1 tsp pure vanilla extract

200g (7oz) rolled
   (old-fashioned)
   porridge oats

200g (7oz) self-raising
   (self-rising) flour

2 tsp baking powder

60g (2oz) coconut sugar
   or soft brown sugar

2 tsp ground cinnamon

125ml (4fl oz) milk of
   your choice*

200g (7oz) blueberries

12-hole muffin tin, lined
   with muffin cases

Preheat the oven to 180°C fan (200°C/400°F/Gas 6).

Mash the bananas with a fork in a large bowl, then whisk in the eggs, butter and vanilla.

Now add the rest of the ingredients, except for the blueberries, and stir well to combine. Fold in three-quarters of the blueberries.

Spoon the mixture into the muffin cases in the muffin tin and top with the remaining blueberries.

Bake in the preheated oven for 20–25 minutes until a skewer comes out clean when inserted into the centre of one of the muffins. Transfer to a wire rack to cool before digging in.

Store the muffins in an airtight container at room temperature for 2–3 days, or freeze for up to 3 months.

1, 2, 3 BABY BANANA PANCAKES

GF

EF*

V

Vg*

DF

As easy as 1, 2, 3 – these scrummy little pancakes are incredibly simple to make and can be whipped up in under 10 minutes. They are also perfectly soft in texture for babies from 6 months, making them ideal weaning food.

🍴 **15 little pancakes**
⏱ **10 minutes**

1 banana
2 eggs or 2 tbsp chia
  seeds, see below*
3 heaped tbsp rolled
  (old-fashioned)
  porridge oats
sunflower oil, coconut oil
  or unsalted butter, for
  frying

Mash the banana in a high-sided plate, using the back of a fork. Toddlers may enjoy helping with this bit – don't worry if there are a few lumps! Add the eggs and whisk into the banana with the fork. Measure the oats into the bowl and mix well.

Heat a non-stick frying pan with a little of your chosen oil or butter over a high heat. Once you can feel the pan is hot enough when hovering your hand over it, reduce the heat down to medium.

Spoon tablespoonfuls of the mixture onto the pan and, using the spoon, neaten and even out each pancake into little circles. Depending on the size of your pan, cook them in batches of around 5 pancakes. Fry for 1–2 minutes before flipping. To do this, grab a thin and sturdy spatula and quickly slide it under the pancake to flip over. Cook for a further minute until both sides are nicely coloured and the pancake has hardened.

Serve with yogurt of your choice* for dipping and fresh fruit on the side, if you like.

Store the pancakes in an airtight container in the fridge for 2 days, or freeze layered between pieces of baking paper for up to 3 months.

MAKE IT EGG-FREE!
To make this recipe egg-free, once the banana has been mashed, add 2 tbsp chia seeds and 5 tbsp warm water, stir and mix in the oats. Let the mixture rest for 10 minutes before frying.

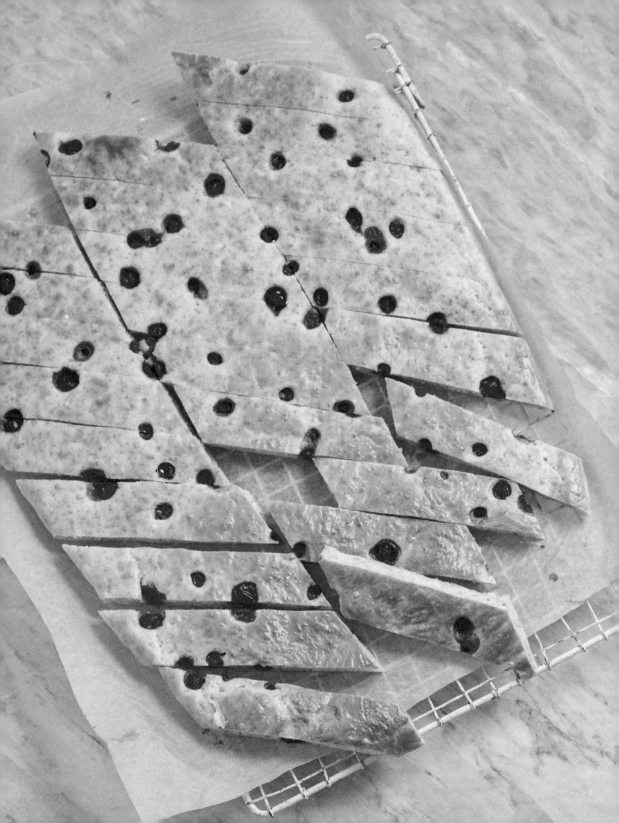

SHEET PAN PANCAKES

You're about to begin flipping pancakes when baby starts to cry! Worry not, just pour the mixture onto a lined baking tray and bung it in the oven!

EF*

V

Vg*

DF*

2 adults and 2 littles
15 minutes

200g (7oz) plain
  (all-purpose) flour
70g (2½oz) rolled
  (old-fashioned)
  porridge oats
2 tsp baking powder
260ml (9fl oz) milk of
  your choice*
3 eggs or 3 chia eggs, see
  page 140*
1 tsp pure vanilla extract
100–150g (3½–5¼oz)
  berries

Preheat the oven to 180°C fan (200°C/400°F/Gas 6).

Measure out all the ingredients except the fruit into a large bowl and mix well to combine, but be sure not to over-mix the batter Pour onto a lined baking tray and scatter over the fruit evenly.

Bake for 10–13 minutes until puffed up, cooked in the middle and the fruit has started to release its juices. Cut into fingers to serve.

Store in the fridge for 2 days or freeze for up to 3 months. To reheat from frozen, microwave on high for 90–120 seconds, flipping halfway through. Ensure the pancakes are piping hot before allowing to cool and serving.

BLUEBERRY PANCAKE BITES

Soft little pillows crammed full of sweet, vitamin C-rich blueberries. A fuss-free alternative to a traditional pancake stack. Pictured page 2.

EF*

V

Vg*

DF*

24 mini bites
15 minutes

150g (5½oz) blueberries
2 eggs or 2 tbsp ground
  flaxseeds (linseeds)
  mixed with an extra
  75ml (2½fl oz) milk*
150g (5½oz) plain
  (all-purpose) flour
1½ tsp baking powder
140ml (4¾oz) milk of
  your choice*
24-hole silicone mini
  muffin mould

Preheat the oven to 200°C fan (220°C/425°F/Gas 7).

Roughly chop 100g (3½oz) of the blueberries and set aside.

Mix together the eggs, flour, baking powder and milk in a bowl. Fold in the chopped blueberries.

Fill each hole of the mini muffin mould two-thirds of the way up. Top each section with the remaining whole blueberries.

Bake in the preheated oven for 10–15 minutes until the bites have puffed up and are golden on top.

These pancake bites will keep in the fridge for a couple of days or freeze for up to 3 months.

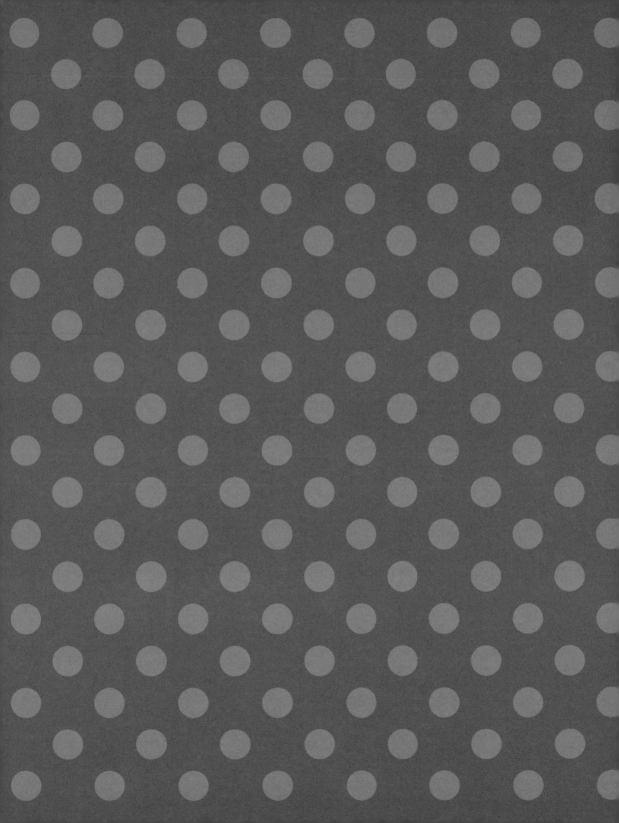

Lunch

QUICK FLATBREADS

EF

V

Vg*

DF*

Flatbreads are such a versatile carb option, great for dunking, wrapping and rolling! Quickly whip up a batch to keep you going through the week. You can serve them alongside curries, stews or soups, wrap them around lunch fillings, or top them with your favourite pizza flavours and pop into a hot oven for a quick-and-easy midweek dinner that everyone will love!

🍴 **10 flatbreads**
⏱ **20 minutes**

300g (10oz) self-raising (self-rising) flour, plus extra for dusting
300g (10oz) full-fat Greek-style yogurt or plant-based alternative*
1 tsp baking powder

Add all the ingredients to a bowl and stir until the mixture starts to come together. Tip out onto a clean work surface and knead the dough for around 60 seconds until a smooth ball has formed. Cut into 10 sections.

Put a frying pan or griddle pan over a high heat to warm up while you roll the first flatbread.

Dust your work surface and rolling pin with some extra flour, then take the first piece of dough, and roll out as thinly as you can, ideally around 2–3mm (⅛in) thick. Keep moving the dough and dusting with flour as you go to ensure the flatbread doesn't stick to the surface or rolling pin.

Shake off any excess flour and put the flatbread in the hot pan. Once you see large bubbles forming on the dough (this will take 1–2 minutes), flip with tongs and cook on the other side for a minute until char marks appear.

Place on a plate or board and cover with a clean tea towel to keep warm while you make the rest.

Once cool, store in an airtight container or bag for up to 5 days. If the flat breads have turned a little hard and stale, splash with some water and reheat at 180°C fan (200°C/400°F/Gas 6) for a couple of minutes until warm and soft.

You can freeze these for up to 3 months. Defrost thoroughly and reheat in the oven or microwave briefly until piping hot.

HUMMUS AND BABY-FRIENDLY DUNKERS

Chickpeas are full of protein and paired with nutty tahini paste, hummus is a total winner for babies and adults alike! My Nina calls it "dip-dip", and there are many things you can dunk into it. You can even coat a bowl of freshly cooked pasta with a dollop of homemade hummus for a speedy dinner!

🍴 **1 adult and 2 littles**
⏱ **2 minutes**

HUMMUS
400g can chickpeas, drained
2 small garlic cloves, roughly chopped
2 tsp olive oil
juice of 1 lemon, plus extra to serve
pinch each of smoked paprika and ground cumin (optional)
1 tbsp tahini (sesame seed paste)
freshly ground black pepper
garlic-infused olive oil, to serve

DUNKERS
toast fingers
breadsticks
pitta bread strips
avocado fingers
cucumber fingers
cooked vegetable fingers, such as carrot and courgette (zucchini)
quick flatbreads, see opposite (optional*)

Add all the ingredients to a food processor with 2 tbsp cold tap water and a good grinding of black pepper, and whizz up until super smooth. Add a little extra splash of water if you prefer a looser consistency.

Serve with an optional tiny drizzle of garlic-infused olive oil, a little ground black pepper and freshly squeezed lemon juice. Serve with your choice of dunkers or simply spread on a rice cake or slice of bread and dig in!

This will keep covered in the fridge for up to 7 days or the freezer for up to 4 months.

NUTRITION NOTE
Iron stores start to run low from around 6 months of age, so it is important to include iron-rich foods, such as meat, fish, eggs, beans and pulses in your child's diet on a very regular (if not daily) basis. Chickpeas are packed full of iron, making this hummus a winner for baby and family!

3-MINUTE PASTA SAUCE

EF

V

Vg*

DF*

Pushed for time and need a super-quick meal with minimal effort? Try this smokey tomato and herb pasta sauce – ready in just 3 minutes! This is perfect for lunch or dinner, and is even a winner in packed lunch boxes, served hot or cold.

🍴 1 adult and 1 little
⏲ 5 minutes

125g (4½oz) dried
  quick-cook penne
large handful of frozen
  peas or broccoli,
  chopped into small
  florets
1½ tbsp tomato purée
  (paste)
1 tsp garlic purée (paste),
  or 1 garlic clove,
  crushed
½ tsp mixed dried herbs
1 tsp smoked paprika
50g (1¾oz) grated
  Cheddar or 1 heaped
  tbsp nutritional yeast*
freshly ground black
  pepper
a few basil leaves, to
  garnish (optional)

Bring a pan of water to the boil and add the pasta and peas or broccoli. Cook for 5 minutes or according to the pasta packet instructions.

Meanwhile, in a medium microwavable bowl, combine the tomato purée, garlic purée, grated cheese, mixed herbs, smoked paprika and a pinch of black pepper. Stir well.

Add 2 ladlefuls of the pasta cooking water – about 150ml (5fl oz) – and give it a good mix. If you have a microwave, give it a blast for 2 minutes, as this will give a silkier finish. However, you can skip this step if you don't have one – it'll still be yummy!

Once the pasta and veg are cooked, drain and stir through the sauce quickly while the pasta is still piping hot. Serve with an extra grating of cheese, and a few basil leaves, to garnish.

TOP TIP
Use nutritional yeast as a dairy free substitute for cheese. Although it won't melt like dairy cheese, it will add a savoury cheesy taste to your meal, as well as adding extra protein, vitamins and minerals to the dish.

CHEESY SWEET POTATO AND CARROT ROSTI

Rostis are usually made with white potato, which gives a delicious but hard-to-eat texture for little ones. Sweet potato and carrot are much softer.

🍴 6 rosti
⏱ 10 minutes

1 sweet potato, peeled and finely grated
1 large carrot, peeled and finely grated
60g (2oz) Cheddar, grated (optional*)
1 tsp smoked paprika
1 garlic clove, crushed
1 tbsp plain (all-purpose) flour
1 tbsp groundnut oil
freshly ground black pepper

In batches, take handfuls of the grated sweet potato and carrot, and squeeze out as much moisture as possible. Do this over the sink to catch the liquid as an unexpected amount will come out. You can also use a clean tea towel to squeeze out the liquid. Add the veg to a bowl with the rest of the ingredients (except the oil) and a good grinding of black pepper. Stir well to combine.

Heat the oil in a large non-stick frying pan, then add small tablespoonfuls of the mixture. Try to form rough round patties and flatten with the back of the spoon to about 1cm (½in) thick.

Fry for 2–3 minutes on each side, then set aside on a piece of kitchen paper. Repeat until all the mixture is used up. Cut into strips to serve, with yogurt of your choice*, for dipping.

These rostis will keep for 2 days in the fridge, or 3 months in the freezer. Reheat in the microwave or oven until piping hot inside.

CHEESY CAULIFLOWER PATTIES

Cauliflower can have quite a strong veggie taste, but turning it into these delicious soft cauliflower patties will please even your fussiest eaters.

🍴 12 patties
⏱ 10 minutes

1 small cauliflower
1 garlic clove
1 egg or 1 chia egg, see page 140*
170g (6oz) self-raising (self-rising) flour
90g (3oz) Cheddar
100ml (3½fl oz) full-fat (whole) milk
1 tsp baking powder
black pepper
olive oil, for cooking

Remove the florets from the cauliflower stalk, and add to a food processor along with the garlic clove. Whizz up until the cauliflower resembles fine breadcrumbs.

Add the rest of the ingredients with a good grinding of black pepper, and blend until just combined. Try not to over-mix.

Heat a large non-stick frying pan over a medium heat with a little drizzle of oil. Take slightly heaped tablespoonfuls of the mixture and dollop into the pan, ensuring the patties aren't touching each other – you should be able to do about 5 at a time. Gently smooth into a rough circle shape, and cook for about 2 minutes on each side until nicely golden on the outside and cooked all the way through in the middle. Repeat until the mixture is used up.

Cut into strips if serving to baby.

TORTILLA ROLL-UPS

Spread this scrummy cheese savoury mixture across a fresh tortilla wrap, roll up and slice into sweet baby-sized pinwheels. Great for eating on the go, family lunches or even party platters.

Vg*
DF*

🍴 **30 bite-sized roll-ups**
⏱ **10 minutes**

15cm (6in) piece of cucumber
1 carrot
50g (1¾oz) full-fat cream cheese or plant-based alternative*
40g (1½oz) full-fat Greek-style yogurt or plant-based alternative*
½ tsp garlic powder
50g (1¾oz) Double Gloucester cheese, grated or any plant-based hard cheese you prefer*
1 tbsp finely chopped chives
1 tsp black or white sesame seeds
4 large tortilla wraps
freshly ground black pepper

Lay a clean tea towel on your work surface, and place a box grater in the centre. Wash and coarsely grate the cucumber and carrot (removing any woody ends; there is no need to peel). Gather the ends of the tea towel together and squeeze over a sink or bowl, removing as much moisture as you can from the veg.

Add to a large bowl, along with the cream cheese, yogurt, garlic powder, grated cheese, chives, sesame seeds and some freshly ground black pepper. Stir to mix well.

Lay a tortilla flatbread on your surface, spread with a couple of tablespoons of the mixture in a thin, even layer, and you cannot see any tortilla underneath which isn't covered with the mixture. Make sure you go edge-to-edge.

Tightly roll up the rest. At this point you can wrap up and store in the fridge for up to 2 days, until you wish to serve. The longer you leave it, the softer the pinwheels will be.

When ready to eat, cut into 2cm (¾in) rounds.

TORTILLA OR PITTA PIZZA

Have a little fridge raid, and empty the contents of the veg drawer onto a tortilla wrap or pitta, top with cheese and bake until crispy around the edges, but cheesy and oozy in the middle.

EF

V*

Vg*

DF*

🍴 **1 adult and 2 littles**
⏱ **15 minutes**

5 mini pitta breads or
   2 regular pitta breads
   or 4 mini tortilla
   wraps or 2 regular
   tortilla wraps

SAUCE
2 tbsp tomato purée
   (paste)
1 tsp garlic-infused olive
   oil
½ tsp mixed dried herbs
½ tsp smoked paprika
freshly ground black
   pepper

TOPPING
70g (2½oz) Cheddar
   or vegan cheese*,
   grated, plus your
   choice of toppings,
   see below

Preheat the oven to 180°C fan (200°C/400°F/Gas 6).

Mix the sauce ingredients together with 4 tbsp cold water, then spread over your desired base, leaving a 1cm (½in) rim around the edge.

Place the bases onto a large baking tray, then spread over your desired toppings evenly along with a good sprinkling of cheese. Try not to use too many toppings, as this makes the pizzas a little soggy and difficult to cook through evenly.

Pop on the middle shelf of the preheated oven and bake for about 10–15 minutes until the cheese has melted and the base has started to turn golden around the edges.

FAMILY-FRIENDLY TOPPING OPTIONS

- cherry tomatoes, quartered
- (bell) pepper, thinly sliced
- ham, chopped (optional*)
- frozen spinach, defrosted and drained
- mushrooms, thinly sliced
- canned sweetcorn
- broccoli, blanched and finely chopped
- cooked chicken, shredded

- leftover minced beef ragu, see page 51 (optional*)
- leftover lentil spag bol, see page 156
- onion, thinly sliced
- sliced olives, rinsed to remove excess brine (in moderation as olives can be on the salty side)

QUESADILLA THREE WAYS

Quesadillas are a great finger food for little ones. Melty, oozy cheese,
nutritious fillings and a crispy tortilla on the outside holding it all together.

SMOKEY BEAN

🍴 **1 adult and 2 littles**
⏱ **10 minutes**

400g can mixed beans in
   water (ensure no
   added salt), drained
   and rinsed (shake off
   any excess water)
100g (3½oz) smoked
   Cheddar or vegan
   cheese*, grated
1 tsp smoked paprika
1 tsp garlic granules
2 large tortilla wraps
black pepper

In a large flat-bottomed bowl, mash the beans with a potato masher to a lumpy paste. Stir in the cheese, paprika, garlic and some black pepper.

Place a large dry frying pan over a medium heat. As it is coming up to temperature, place one tortilla in the pan. Spoon half the filling onto one half of the tortilla, then fold over to enclose.

Add the second tortilla to the pan, and repeat with the remaining mixture, folding over so the straight side of the quesadilla is down the centre of the pan, and the two wraps are sitting snuggly together. Press them, so the mixture is compacted neatly.

Cook for 4–5 minutes on each side, flipping once the underneath has started to turn golden. If it's browning too quickly, turn down the heat. You want the filling to go oozy and melty before the tortilla has had a chance to burn. Cool for a couple of minutes and cut into wedges to serve.

APPLE, COURGETTE AND CHEESE

🍴 **1 adult and 2 littles**
⏱ **10 minutes**

10cm (4in) piece of
   courgette (zucchini),
   coarsely grated
1 apple, coarsely grated
80g (3oz) Cheddar or
   vegan cheese*, grated
2 large tortilla wraps

Gather the grated courgette and apple in your hands and squeeze out the liquid. Add to a bowl with the cheese, and mix together.

Place a large dry frying pan over a medium heat. As it is coming up to temperature, place one tortilla in the pan. Spoon half the mixture onto one half of the tortilla, then fold over to enclose.

Add the second tortilla to the pan, and repeat with the remaining mixture, folding over so the straight side of the quesadilla is down the centre of the pan, and the two wraps are sitting snuggly together. Press them, so the mixture is compacted neatly.

Cook for 4–5 minutes on each side, flipping once the underneath has started to turn golden. If it's browning too quickly, turn down the heat. Cool for a few minutes and cut into wedges to serve.

TUNA AND AVO

EF

🍴 **1 adult and 2 littles**
⏱ **15 minutes**

2 small avocados
1 garlic clove, finely
    chopped
juice of ½ lemon
145g can tuna in
    spring-water, drained
4 tbsp drained canned
    sweetcorn
2 tbsp full-fat Greek-style
    yogurt
40g (1½oz) cheese, grated
2 large tortilla wraps
freshly ground black
    pepper

Preheat the oven to 200°C fan (220°C/425°F/Gas 7).

Mash the avocado flesh with the back of a fork and add to a flat-bottomed bowl with the garlic, lemon juice and a good grinding of black pepper. Mash together with the back of a fork. Now add the tuna, sweetcorn and yogurt, and give it a good stir.

Place one tortilla on a baking tray and sprinkle over a little cheese. Spread the avo-tuna mixture evenly over the tortilla and cover with the rest of the cheese. Top with the second tortilla.

Bake in the preheated oven for 10–15 minutes until crispy on top and all the cheese has melted inside. Cool for a couple of minutes and cut into wedges using a pizza wheel.

ALL ABOUT BREAD
Whilst wholemeal foods like brown bread are safe to offer babies, they do tend to fill up their tummies quickly, running the risk that baby won't get all the nutrients they need in their diet. Therefore it's best to offer wholegrain foods in moderation.

CHEESE TOASTIES TWO WAYS

EF

V

Two 10-minute recipes for simple lunches that you and your little one will love to share. The humble cheese toastie has a new friend in the form of nutritious, vitamin C-packed avocado – an unlikely pairing that works really well. You gotta try this one! And then I add in some extra veggies in the delicious carrot, chive and cheese combo!

AVO CHEESE TOASTIE

🍴 **1 adult and 1 little**
⏱ **10 minutes**

1 small avocado
juice of ½ lemon
30g (1oz) Cheddar, thinly
    sliced
2 slices of white bread,
    see opposite
2 tsp unsalted butter,
    softened
freshly ground black
    pepper

Remove the skin and stone (pit) of the avocado. Mash the flesh with the lemon juice and a good grinding of black pepper. Spread the mixture over a slice of bread, ensuring you reach all the edges. Top with the cheese and the second piece of bread.

Heat a griddle pan over a medium heat. Spread butter edge-to-edge on the top side of the bread, then pop the sandwich onto the pan, buttered-side down. Spread butter on the other side of the sandwich, and fry for a couple of minutes before flipping. Cook until crispy and golden on the outside, but oozy and melty on the inside.

CARROT, CHIVE AND CHEESE TOASTIE

🍴 **1 adult and 1 little**
⏱ **10 minutes**

1 carrot, finely grated
35g (1¼oz) Cheddar,
    grated
1½ tsp finely chopped
    chives
2 slices of white bread,
    see opposite
1 tbsp full-fat cream
    cheese
2 tsp unsalted butter,
    softened
freshly ground black
    pepper

Gather the grated carrot in your hands and squeeze out the juice. Add to a bowl. Add the grated cheese, the chives and a pinch of black pepper, and mix well.

Take one piece of bread and spread half of the cream cheese over one side. Evenly distribute the carrot and cheese mixture over the top, pressing down to compact the mixture together. Spread the rest of the cream cheese over the second piece of bread and place on top of the carrot mixture, cream cheese-side down.

Heat a griddle pan over a medium heat. Spread soft butter edge-to-edge on the top side of the bread, then pop the sandwich onto the pan, buttered-side down. Spread butter on the other side of the sandwich, and fry for a couple of minutes before flipping. Cook until crispy and golden on the outside, but oozy and melty on the inside.

CHICKEN NOODLE SOUP

This Hungarian chicken soup is adapted from my wonderful mother's recipe, she's been serving it to me since I was a little girl. I was delivered a big pot of it when Nina was born, and now she makes it for us all when we go to visit. Whether baby has got the sniffles and is all bunged up, you all need warming up on a winter's day, or you just want a bowl full of delicious nutrition, this soup is my go-to!

DF

EF*

🍴 2 adults and 2 littles
⏱ 25 minutes

500g (1lb 2oz) chicken thighs, see below
1 carrot, peeled and cut into large wedges
1 onion, peeled but left whole
1 tsp coriander seeds
2–3 juniper berries (optional)
2 whole cloves (optional)
3–4 whole allspice (optional)
2 garlic cloves
6–7 whole black peppercorns
¼ whole nutmeg
1cm (½in) piece of ginger, or ½ tsp ground ginger)
nests of egg noodles or other thick, egg-free noodles*

Add all the ingredients to a large saucepan and add just enough boiling water to cover everything by about 2.5cm (1in).

Simmer for 20–25 minutes until the chicken is cooked and the carrots are tender.

Meanwhile cook some thick egg noodles and set aside until the broth is ready.

To serve, place cooked noodles in each bowl, shred a little chicken into the bowl, layer over the carrots and then ladle over the broth using a sieve (strainer) to catch the seeds. You can also serve the broth in an open or sippy cup for baby, with the veggies and noodles on a side plate. Lots of different tastes and textures in one meal, a fantastic sensory experience for baby!

You may find this soup needs salt to bring out the flavour, so feel free to add this to your portion at the table and leave out the salt for baby.

The strained broth is freezable for up to 3 months. Use as a chicken stock once defrosted.

PACKED WITH FLAVOUR!
Buy chicken thighs with the bone in and skin on, but remove the skin before cooking as it releases too much fat into the broth. Keeping the bone in adds flavour to the soup.

LEMON AND GARLIC PRAWN ORZO

EF

Full of fresh and summery flavours, this quick dish – ready in under 15 minutes – is a great way to serve seafood to baby. Always ensure the prawns are fully cooked before serving by opening one up to check it is fully pink all the way through and has a firm texture.

🍴 2 adults and 2 littles
⏱ 15 minutes

250g (9oz) dried orzo
150g (5½oz) frozen peas
1 tsp garlic-infused or
  regular olive oil
30g (1oz) unsalted butter
300g (10oz) raw king
  prawns (jumbo
  shrimp), see below
1 large lemon, halved
2 garlic cloves, grated
1 heaped tsp finely
  chopped curly parsley
freshly ground black
  pepper

Bring a pan of water to the boil and add the orzo. Cook for 5 minutes, then add the peas to the pan, stir and let it all cook for a further 5–6 minutes.

Heat a large non-stick frying pan over a medium-high heat, and add the olive oil and half the butter. Once melted, add the prawns and garlic, stirring occasionally. Once the prawns are pink, firm and piping hot all the way through, squeeze the juice of most of the lemon into the pan. Reserve the lemon for an extra squeeze of juice at the end.

Add the chopped parsley and the rest of the butter. Gather half a ladleful of the pasta cooking water and add to the prawn pan, giving it all a good stir. Season with black pepper.

Reserve some of the pasta cooking water in a mug, then drain the pasta and peas, and add to the prawn pan. Mix everything together and add an extra splash of the pasta water if you need to loosen the sauce.

Serve with an extra squeeze of lemon juice and a little black pepper on top. Adults, you may want to season your portion with salt at the table.

TOP TIP
Large king prawns are a good finger food for baby, suitable from 6 months. However, if you can only find smaller prawns, chop them up finely and stir them into the pasta for baby.

CHEESY BROCCOLI ORZO

EF

V

Vg*

DF*

This cheesy orzo pasta with broccoli is creamy and oozy, and super quick to prepare in under 10 minutes! It is suitable from 6 months, but if serving to babies younger than 9 months, mash the broccoli pieces before serving to them.

⫴ 2 adults and 1 little
⏱ 10 minutes

200g (7oz) dried orzo
160g (5½oz) broccoli,
   chopped into small
   florets
100g (3½oz) full-fat
   cream cheese or
   dairy-free cream
   cheese or thick
   coconut cream*
1 tbsp garlic-infused olive
   oil, or regular olive oil
   mixed with 1 crushed
   garlic clove
90g (3oz) grated Cheddar
   or 2 tbsp nutritional
   yeast* (optional)
freshly ground black
   pepper

Bring a pan of water to the boil and add the pasta. Cook according to the packet instructions, and add the broccoli florets to the pasta cooking water when there is 5 minutes left of cooking.

Using a mug, scoop out some of the pasta water and set aside. Drain the pasta and broccoli, and add back into the pan. Add the cream cheese, garlic-infused oil, grated cheese, a good grinding of black pepper and a splash of the reserved cooking water. Give it a good stir and serve!

With this shape of pasta you can either give pre-loaded spoonfuls to baby, spoon-feed them yourself, or let baby get stuck in with their fingers to taste and feel it themselves. As the pasta cools it will clump up a little, making it easier to hold.

Store in the fridge for up to 2 days or freeze for up to 3 months. Defrost and reheat with a splash of water to loosen.

LEMON AND GARLIC
PRAWN ORZO,
SEE PAGE 58

CREAMY LEEK PASTA

Ready in the time it takes to cook the pasta, this super creamy, veg-filled meal will be a hit with the whole family. For children who need a wheat-free or gluten-free diet, try a lentil or pea pasta instead.

EF

V*

Vg*

DF*

🍴 **2 adults and 2 littles**
⏱ **15 minutes**

250g (9oz) dried pasta
2 leeks
15g (½oz) unsalted butter
   (optional*)
drizzle of olive oil
½ garlic clove, crushed
1 low-salt chicken or
   vegetable stock cube*
100ml (3½fl oz) single
   (light) cream or
   coconut, soya or oat
   cream or dairy-free
   cream cheese*
100g (3½oz) grated
   Cheddar or 1 tbsp
   nutritional yeast*,
   plus extra to serve
freshly ground black
   pepper

Bring a pan of water to the boil and add the pasta. Cook for about 11 minutes or according to the packet instructions.

Trim the tough dark green end off the leek about 2.5cm (1in) from the end. Then cut a line down the centre of the leek, keeping the root still attached. Wash the leeks under running water with the root facing upwards. This allows the muddy water to escape.

Heat a large non-stick frying pan over a medium heat and add the butter and olive oil.

Meanwhile thinly slice the leeks about 5mm (¼in) thick, discarding the root. Once the butter has melted, add the leeks to the pan, and give it a good stir. Then add the crushed garlic, crumble in the stock cube and add a pinch of freshly ground black pepper.

Allow the leeks to wilt down, stirring often. Occasionally add a ladle of the pasta cooking water to help the leeks break down.

Once the leeks are really soft, add the cream and cheese, and give it a good stir until the cheese has melted into the sauce. Add a splash more of the cooking water if the sauce is still too thick.

Drain the cooked pasta and add to the leeks. Stir well and serve with an extra grating of cheese on top. Babies can eat this dish as finger food, but you can also roughly blend the pasta and sauce to a lumpy purée for baby. This can be done with all pasta dishes.

TIME-SAVING TIP
See page 216 for my time-saving cooking tips and tricks, including how to quickly bring a pot of pasta water to the boil, and how to minimise the risk of it boiling over.

FOUR QUICK PASTAS

For quick-and-easy meals, these recipes are all tried-and-tested crowd-pleasers. Choose large pasta shapes that are easy for baby to hold.

🍴 **2 adults and 2 littles**
⏲ **15-30 minutes**

THREE-CHEESE PASTA BAKE

250g (9oz) dried pasta
150g (5½oz) frozen peas
140g (5oz) mascarpone
90g (3oz) full-fat cream
    cheese
50ml (1¾fl oz) full-fat
    (whole) milk
140g (5oz) Cheddar,
    grated
freshly ground black
    pepper

Preheat the oven to 220°C fan (240°C/475°F/Gas 9).

Bring a pan of water to the boil and add the ditali. Cook according to the packet instructions, but add the peas to the pasta cooking water when there is 5 minutes left of cooking.

Meanwhile, in a large bowl, mix together the mascarpone, cream cheese, milk, 80g (3oz) of the grated cheese and a good grinding of black pepper.

Drain the pasta and peas, add to the bowl and combine, then pour the mixture into an ovenproof dish. Top with the remaining grated cheese and a little more freshly ground black pepper.

Bake in the preheated oven for 15–20 minutes or until the cheese has melted and turned a gorgeous golden colour.

SPINACH PESTO PASTA

250g (9oz) dried pasta
large handful of basil
2 large handfuls of baby
    leaf spinach
1 large garlic clove,
    roughly chopped
2 tbsp olive oil
juice of ½ large lemon
handful of pine nuts
    (optional)
large handful of grated
    Cheddar
freshly ground black
    pepper

Bring a pan of water to the boil and add the pasta. Cook according to the packet instructions.

Meanwhile, place the rest of the ingredients into a blender with a ladleful of the pasta cooking water, about 200ml (7fl oz). Whizz up until smooth. If you prefer a looser consistency, add a little more water.

Drain the pasta and mix with the pesto. Serve with an extra grinding of cheese.

Any leftover pesto which hasn't been mixed with pasta yet will freeze really well. Pop into an ice cube tray to freeze in portions. Defrost and stir through freshly cooked pasta.

CREAMY TOMATO PASTA

250g (9oz) dried pasta
500g (1lb 2oz) rustic
   crushed tomatoes or
   good-quality passata
   (strained tomatoes)
1 tbsp tomato purée
   (paste)
1 tsp dried basil
1 tbsp Worcestershire
   sauce (optional*)
1 tsp garlic granules, or
   1 garlic clove, crushed
1 tsp smoked paprika
1 low-salt vegetable or
   chicken stock cube*
150ml (5½oz) single
   (light) cream
   (optional*)
freshly ground black
   pepper

Bring a pan of water to the boil and add the pasta. Cook according to the packet instructions.

Meanwhile, In a separate lidded saucepan, add the tomatoes or passata, tomato purée, dried basil, Worcestershire sauce, garlic, smoked paprika and a good grinding of black pepper, and crumble in the stock cube. Give it all a good stir and bring to a gentle simmer, half-covering with a lid to allow it to reduce.

Simmer the sauce for 4 minutes, then add the cream (if using), stir and place the lid back on as above. Let the sauce simmer for another 4 minutes until the pasta is cooked. The cream is optional, but it does add a silkier texture and helps cut through the acidity in the tomatoes without needing to add sugar.

Drain the pasta and stir it through the sauce. Serve with an extra grinding of black pepper. Adults you may want to season your plate with a little salt, if desired. Serve with salad or boiled veg.

MAKE A BATCH!
This recipe makes a big batch of sauce, so if you prefer your pasta dishes to be a little more dry, freeze one-third of the sauce for up to 3 months. Defrost and warm up until piping hot.

TOMATO AND TUNA PASTA

EF

1 tbsp garlic-infused olive
   oil
1 small onion, finely diced
2 garlic cloves, crushed
145g can tuna in spring
   water
400g can chopped
   tomatoes
small bunch of basil,
   torn, or ½ tsp dried
1 tsp smoked paprika
2 tsp Worcestershire sauce
250g (9oz) dried pasta
freshly ground black
   pepper
Cheddar, grated, to serve

Put a saucepan over a medium-high heat and add the garlic-infused olive oil. Add the onion and sauté for 4 minutes, stirring often, until the onion has turned translucent. Add the garlic and tuna to the pan (including the spring water in the tin), and cook for a minute before adding the tomatoes. Add the basil, smoked paprika, Worcestershire sauce and a good grinding of black pepper, stir and pop the lid on to simmer for 10–15 minutes.

Meanwhile, cook the pasta according to the packet instructions. Drain the pasta and stir into the sauce. Serve topped with grated Cheddar while still hot, so the cheese melts into the sauce.

NUTRITION NOTE
Try to find tuna in spring water as this has a much lower salt content than brine.

Dinner

HULK MAC 'N' CHEESE

Pimp up your macaroni cheese with nutritious spinach – a great way to get extra veggies into your fussy eater. This can be whipped up in under 10 minutes – a speedy lunch or dinner any time. It's my Nina's favourite!

EF

V

Vg*

DF*

🍴 **2 adults and 2 littles**
⏱ **10 minutes**

250g (9oz) dried macaroni (or any pasta shape will work)
140g (5oz) frozen chopped spinach (about 7 blocks)
500ml (16fl oz) milk of your choice*
100g (3½oz) grated Cheddar or 2 tbsp nutritional yeast*
1 tbsp unsalted butter or dairy free spread or coconut oil*
2 tbsp cornflour (cornstarch)
freshly ground black pepper

Bring a pan of water to the boil and add the pasta. Cook according to the packet instructions.

To a microwaveable jug, add the frozen spinach and milk. Cook for 3 minutes until the spinach is nearly defrosted and the milk slightly warmed.

In a hot frying pan, melt the butter then add cornflour. Stir and cook for a minute, then add the spinach milk gradually, whisking continuously. Stir until the sauce is thickened. Remove the pan from the heat and add a good grinding of black pepper and the grated cheese. Stir to melt the cheese into the sauce then set aside until the pasta is cooked.

Add the drained, cooked pasta to the sauce, stir and serve with an extra grating of cheese on top, if you like.

Any leftovers will keep for a couple of days. Spoon them into an ovenproof dish, top with more cheese and bake for 15–20 minutes for a delicious pasta bake. Alternatively, if you're thinking ahead, make extra sauce and reserve some of it before mixing with the pasta. Freeze in portions for up to 3 months for a quick pasta sauce on days when you're feeling rushed. Defrost in the microwave with an extra splash of milk until piping hot, before stirring through freshly cooked pasta.

TIP
To use fresh spinach you'll need to finely chop around 3 handfuls of spinach and add to the sauce in the pan at the same time as the grated cheese, rather than in the microwave.

CHEESY SQUASH PASTA

Delicious mac and cheese vibes, but packed full of veg, and ready in just 10 minutes! Choose a nice long pasta shape like fusilli, which is easy for young babies to hold.

EF

V

Vg*

DF*

🍴 **2 adults and 1 little**
⏱ **10 minutes**

250g (9oz) dried pasta
350g (12oz) butternut
squash, peeled and cut
into small cubes
1 small garlic clove
100g (3½oz) grated
Cheddar or 2 tbsp
nutritional yeast*
½ tsp smoked paprika
freshly ground black
pepper
chopped chives, to
garnish

Bring a pan of water to the boil and add the pasta. Cook according to the packet instructions.

In a separate pan, boil the squash cubes and peeled garlic clove for 7–8 minutes until soft when a fork is inserted.

Add the garlic and squash to a blender along with the grated cheese, paprika and a pinch of black pepper. Blend until smooth, then stir through the cooked and drained pasta. Garnish with chopped chives to serve.

The sauce can be frozen for up to 3 months. Freeze in portions, and defrost in the microwave with an extra splash of water to help loosen the consistency, then stir through freshly cooked pasta.

CHEAT'S BEEF RAGU

Prep this comforting beef ragu in just 15 minutes for a quick-and-easy midweek meal. Suitable from 6 months, this is a family favourite! It is egg- and dairy-free, but you can add a grating of cheese on top, if you like. Choose a nice large pasta shape that is easy for baby to hold like rigatoni, fusilli or tripoline, and blend some up for baby's first tastes as pictured on the front cover.

EF

DF

2 adults and 2 littles
15 minutes

500g (1lb 2 oz) lean
  minced (ground) beef
250g (9oz) dried pasta
2 tsp smoked paprika
1 garlic clove, crushed
1 low-salt beef stock cube
1 tbsp Worcestershire
  sauce
1 tsp mixed dried herbs
500g (1lb 2 oz) passata
  (strained tomatoes)
1 tsp maple or fruit syrup
  (optional)

Over a medium heat, add the mince to a dry saucepan. Break it up with a wooden spoon and cook until all the meat has browned nicely (this will take around 4 minutes).

Meanwhile, bring a pan of water to the boil and add the pasta. Cook following the packet instructions.

Back to the ragu. Add the smoked paprika, garlic, crumbled beef stock cube, Worcestershire sauce and mixed herbs to the mince, and give it a good stir.

Now add the passata to the mince, then fill up the empty carton with about 150ml (5fl oz) of tap water (roughly one-third of the carton), swirl it around and add this to the pan too. Give it all a good stir and let it simmer away for 10 minutes until your pasta has cooked.

If the sauce is getting too dry and sticking to the bottom of the pan, add some of the pasta cooking water, but bear in mind this sauce is delicious when thick and not too saucy, so be careful not to add too much water.

Once the pasta is cooked, drain and add to the sauce, give it a good stir and serve with some green veg on the side. You can serve it with grated cheese on top, if you do not need it to be dairy-free.

The sauce will keep in the fridge for a couple of days or freeze for up to 3 months. Defrost with an extra splash of water until piping hot and stir through freshly cooked pasta.

SLOW COOK WINNER!
This ragu is delicious cooked in just 15 minutes, but if you have longer, let it simmer away on the hob for up to 2 hours. Better still, pop it in the slow cooker and forget about it until dinner time! Use left overs to make the lasagne roll-ups on page 120.

ONE-PAN LEMON SALMON
WITH COURGETTE AND POTATO WEDGES

So easy to whip together, this one-pan meal has dinner on the table in 30 minutes!

🍴 **2 adults and 2 littles**
⏱ **30 minutes**

3 salmon fillets, about
   120g (4oz) each
450g (1lb) Maris Piper
   potatoes
1 tbsp garlic-infused olive
   oil
2 small courgettes
   (zucchini)
4 large garlic cloves
1 lemon
30g (1oz) unsalted butter
   or dairy free spread*
freshly ground black
   pepper
large baking tray, lined
   with non-stick baking
   paper

Preheat the oven to 200°C fan (220°C/425°F/Gas 7) and take the fish out of the fridge to come up to room temperature.

Peel the potatoes, cut in half lengthways, then cut into 1.5cm (½in) wide wedges. Place onto the lined baking tray, ensuring they are evenly spaced, drizzle the oil over the wedges and place in the top of the oven.

While the potatoes cook, cut the courgettes in half, then each half into quarters lengthways. After 5 minutes of the potatoes cooking, remove the tray and use a spatula to flip the spuds. Add the courgette slices and the garlic cloves (still with their skin on) and return to the oven for another 5 minutes.

Meanwhile, cut the lemon in half, then cut three nice thin slices from the edge of each half. Squeeze the juice of the remaining lemon into a microwavable bowl, then add the butter and a good grinding of black pepper, and microwave on high for 40 seconds to melt the butter.

Once the courgettes have had 5 minutes and the potatoes 10 minutes, take the tray out of the oven, flip everything and evenly spread out again. Allow a space in the centre of the tray for the salmon, and place the fillets skin-side down onto the tray. Pour the lemon butter over the fish, and place the lemon slices over the salmon.

Put the tray back in the oven for 15 minutes until the fish has cooked fully all the way through. To check this, the salmon should have turned a light pink, easily separate with gentle pressure and when you flake the largest section it should be the same light pink all the way through.

NUTRITION NOTE
Salmon is packed full of essential omega-3 fatty acids and is a fantastic source of protein. A great fish to serve to baby as it flakes away really easily and is super soft, making it much easy for baby to give it a go.

ORANGE AND SOY-GLAZED COD

Citrusy, sweet and tangy, and spiked with Asian flavours, this is a super-quick and delicious method for cooking cod.

🍴 2 adults and 2 littles
⏱ 15 minutes

30g (1oz) unsalted butter
    or dairy free spread*
1 tsp garlic-infused olive
    oil
3 boneless cod fillets,
    about 180g (6oz) each
1 garlic clove, crushed
juice of 1 large orange,
    about 100ml (3½fl oz)
2 tbsp low-salt soy sauce
1 tsp red wine vinegar
1 tbsp cornflour
    (cornstarch)

Heat a large non-stick frying pan over a medium-high heat. Add two-thirds of the butter to the pan along with the garlic-infused oil (this stops the butter from burning). Let the butter melt slightly, then place the fish fillets in the pan, skin-side down. Cook for 9–10 minutes, flipping halfway through. Try not to move the fish between flipping, as this stops you getting a nice crust. Every now and then, tilt the pan and spoon some of the melted butter over the fish (this helps keep the flesh succulent).

Add the cornflour to a small bowl and mix with 1 tbsp of water to make a thick paste. Set aside.

Once the fish is just cooked, remove from the pan and transfer to a plate to rest while you make the sauce.

Add the remaining butter and crushed garlic to the hot pan. Once melted, add the orange juice, soy sauce, red wine vinegar and cornflour paste. Stir and allow to cook for a couple of minutes until it has started to thicken.

Now carefully add the cod back to the pan, trying not to break up the fish, along with any resting juices, and spoon the sauce over the fish. Let it cook for a further minute before serving immediately.

To serve for baby, remove the skin and gently flake the fish into large pieces. This is a good opportunity to look out for any bones that your fishmonger may have missed. Serve with rice or couscous and steamed vegetables.

YOGURT-SPICED FISH BITES

Coating fish in yogurt ensures it stays really soft and succulent, so the flesh flakes really easily when baby digs in.

🍴 2 adults and 2 littles
⏱ 20 minutes

400g (14oz) skinless,
   boneless white fish,
   such as cod or
   haddock
150g (5½oz) full-fat
   Greek-style yogurt
1 tsp garlic granules
2 tsp mild garam masala
½ tsp ground cumin
1 tsp smoked paprika
freshly ground black
   pepper
olive oil cooking spray
baking tray, lined with
   non-stick baking paper

Preheat the oven to 200°C fan (220°C/425°F/Gas 7).

Cut the fish into 3cm (1½in) chunks. Mix the yogurt, spices and a good grinding of black pepper in a bowl until well combined. Add the fish and coat well. Let it sit for a couple of minutes to soak up some of the flavours.

Add the fish to the lined baking tray, ensuring that none of the pieces are touching. Spray each piece with a spray or two of cooking oil spray.

Bake for 10–14 minutes, until the fish is fully cooked and flakes really easily.

Serve with boiled rice, peas and an a wedge of lemon. Or try my smokey wedges from page 81.

MAKE IT FUN!
Mixing the yogurt with the fish is a great job for the little ones to help out with in the kitchen. If it is a struggle to get your little one to enjoy fish or spiced flavours, asking them to help you cook it in the kitchen may help them to be more adventurous when tucking into this dish.

LEMON AND GARLIC SAUTÉED BROCCOLI

Jazz up the simple boiled veg side dish with punchy garlic and citrus flavours.

🍴 2 adults and 2 littles as a side dish
⏱ 10 minutes

1 large head of broccoli, about 400g (14oz), cut into florets
1½ tbsp sesame seeds
1 tsp garlic-infused olive oil
20g (¾oz) unsalted butter or coconut oil*
2 garlic cloves, crushed
finely grated zest of 1 lemon and juice of ½ lemon
freshly ground black pepper

Bring a pan of water to the boil and add the broccoli. Simmer for 4 minutes until just tender.

Meanwhile, heat a large frying pan over a medium heat and add the sesame seeds. Toast for a minute or so until just starting to turn golden. Remove the seeds from the pan and set aside.

Now add the garlic-infused olive oil and butter to the hot pan and allow to melt. Add the crushed garlic and sauté for 30–60 seconds, stirring continuously to ensure the garlic doesn't burn.

Now add the lemon zest and juice, a good grinding of black pepper and two-thirds of the sesame seeds.

Once the veg is cooked, drain well and add to the pan. Sauté for a couple of minutes so all the flavours mingle, then serve with an extra scattering of the remaining toasted sesame seeds.

LEMON AND CHEDDAR CHICKEN BITES

Crispy on the outside and deliciously succulent in the middle. Upgrade your chicken nuggets game, and I bet the whole family will have seconds!

🍴 2 adults, 2 littles (with plenty left for the freezer stash)
🕐 20 minutes

500g (1lb 2oz) boneless, skinless chicken thighs
1 lemon
70g (2½oz) panko breadcrumbs
1 tsp mixed dried herbs
50g (1¾oz) Cheddar, grated (use a good-quality aged Cheddar, if you can find it)
1 heaped tbsp cornflour (cornstarch)
2 eggs
1 tbsp garlic-infused olive oil
freshly ground black pepper

Preheat the oven to 220°C fan (240°C/475°F/Gas 9).

Cut the chicken into 2cm (¾in) wide strips.

Take two large bowls. Zest the lemon into one bowl, then squeeze the juice into the other, making sure no pips sneak in.

To the lemon zest, add the panko breadcrumbs, herbs, a pinch of black pepper and the grated cheese. Stir thoroughly so the breadcrumbs are evenly distributed through the cheese.

Now add the cornflour to the lemon juice and stir until all the flour has dissolved. Crack in the eggs and whisk until everything is combined.

Mix the chicken into the lemon juice and egg mixture, ensuring all the chicken is coated well. Now take a couple of pieces at a time, and add to the breadcrumb mixture, coat well and place onto a non-stick baking tray.

Finally, drizzle the chicken with the garlic-infused oil, and bake for 15–20 minutes until the chicken is golden and crispy, and when sliced open you see no pink meat.

To serve to baby, slice each nugget in half lengthways.

Once baked and cooled, fill up your freezer with a bag of these delicious morsels. Spread the frozen bites on a non-stick baking tray and bake at 180°C fan (200°C/400°F/Gas 6) for 20–25 minutes until piping hot all the way through.

SIMPLE SWAP!
Chicken thighs, cooked in this way, are really succulent. But you can also use breast meat, if you prefer.

TOP TIPS

When coating your chicken, use one hand to handle the wet chicken, and the other to coat in the breadcrumbs. This way you minimize the amount of crumbs stuck to your fingers, rather than the chicken!

Cut steamed corn on the cob into 2cm (¾in) rounds so it's easier for little fingers to hold.

STICKY SESAME ORANGE CHICKEN

With sweet-and-sour vibes, this delicious citrusy chicken dish has all the comforting feels of a Friday night fakeaway!

🍴 2 adults and 2 littles

⏱ 15 minutes

600g (1lb 5oz) chicken breast fillets
1 heaped tbsp cornflour (cornstarch)
1 tbsp groundnut oil, see below
1 red (bell) pepper, sliced into thin strips

SAUCE
finely grated zest of ½ large orange
100ml (3½fl oz) orange juice (roughly the juice of 1 large orange)
1 tsp sesame oil
½ tsp finely grated ginger
1 tbsp apple cider vinegar or any white vinegar
3 tbsp low-salt soy sauce
1 heaped tsp cornflour (cornstarch)
2 garlic cloves, grated
1 tbsp sesame seeds
2 tbsp maple syrup or coconut sugar
juice of ½ lemon
freshly ground black pepper

TO SERVE
1 tsp sesame seeds
1 spring onion (scallion), finely sliced

Cut the chicken into 1cm (½in) wide strips, then pop into a bowl with the cornflour and give it a good mix to coat.

Add the oil to a large non-stick frying pan over a high heat.

Add the chicken pieces to the frying pan in a single layer, so each piece is touching the bottom of the hot pan. Cook for 6–8 minutes, flipping halfway through, until the chicken has turned crispy and golden brown.

While the chicken cooks, add all of the sauce ingredients to a saucepan with 60ml (2fl oz) water and give it a good stir, so the cornflour dissolves into the liquid. Place the pan over a high heat to bring the sauce up to the boil. Once bubbling, lower the heat slightly and let the sauce simmer away until it has thickened and the colour has darkened.

Once the chicken has cooked through, transfer it from the pan to a plate, and set aside. Add the sliced peppers to the hot pan and cook for 5 minutes, stirring often, until softened and cooked through.

Now add the chicken and cooked peppers to the sauce and give it a stir, ensuring that all of the chicken has been coated well.

To serve, top with the sesame seeds and sliced spring onion. Serve with rice or noodles and steamed veg.

NUTRITION NOTE
Groundnut oil is produced using peanuts so proceed with caution when introducing this ingredient to your child's diet. You can easily replace it here with sunflower oil.

SMOKEY SWEET POTATO
AND PARSNIP WEDGES

Add a flavour hit to these veggies, with sweet and smokey paprika.

🍴 **2 adults and 2 littles**

⏱ **30 minutes**

4 large parsnips
5 sweet potatoes
3 tsp smoked paprika
1 tsp garlic granules
3 tsp garlic-infused olive
   oil
freshly ground black
   pepper

Preheat the oven to 200°C fan (220°C/425°F/Gas 7).

Peel the parsnips and sweet potatoes, and cut them into 1cm (½in) wedges. Add the parsnip and sweet potato wedges to a bowl along with the spices, oil and a good grinding of black pepper. Give it all a good toss and stir, then add to a non-stick baking tray.

Bake for 20–25 minutes, or until golden and crispy on the outside, but lovely and soft in the middle. Flip halfway through cooking to ensure the wedges bake evenly.

SATAY CHICKEN DIPPERS

Succulent pieces of chicken, coated in a flavourful peanut sauce.
Make enough for leftovers, as these are delicious cold in sarnies
or packed lunches.

EF

DF

🍴 2 adults and 2 littles

⏲ 20 minutes

500g (1lb 2oz) skinless,
    boneless chicken
    thighs
2 tbsp smooth 100%
    peanut butter
1 tsp garlic granules
1 garlic clove, finely
    grated
2.5cm (1in) piece of
    ginger, peeled and
    finely grated
2 tbsp low-salt soy sauce
finely grated zest and
    juice of 1 lime
2 tbsp honey or maple
    syrup (optional, honey
    is not suitable for
    babies under
    12 months)
1 tsp sesame oil
½ tsp mild curry powder
4 tbsp boiling water
freshly ground black
    pepper
baking tray, lined with
    non-stick baking paper

Preheat the oven to 200°C fan (220°C/425°F/Gas 7).

Cut the chicken into 2cm (¾in) wide strips.

Mix all of the other ingredients together in a jug with a good
grinding of black pepper until super smooth. Pour two-thirds of
the sauce over the chicken, reserving the remaining one-third
of the sauce for dipping.

Toss the chicken well in the sauce, then lay evenly on the lined
baking tray, ensuring none of the pieces of chicken are touching,
as this slows down the cooking time. Bake in the preheated oven
for 15–20 minutes until the chicken has cooked through and is
starting to turn golden on the edges.

Serve with cooked rice, cucumber sticks and the remaining sauce
to dunk the chicken into. For babies under 1, halve each piece of
chicken lengthways so it's easier for baby to hold.

NUTRITION NOTE
It is recommended to serve peanuts to baby from the age of 6
months. Delaying the introduction of peanut or other allergenic
foods may in fact increase your baby's risk of developing
allergies. For more information on how to introduce nuts and
other allergenic foods to baby, see page 208.

GORGEOUS GRAINS CHEAT'S RISOTTO

EF

V

Smooth and creamy peas, jam packed with a glorious array of healthy grains. Traditional risotto takes time to stand and stir at the stove top, which isn't always possible when you have little ones who need your attention. Try my cheat's version, which has the added bonus of nutritious mixed grains helping to offer a wide variety of texture and flavours into your family's diet. Pictured on page 85.

🍴 **3 adults and 2 littles**

⏱ **15 minutes**

1 tbsp sunflower or olive oil

1 white onion, diced

1 large garlic clove, roughly chopped

260g (9oz) frozen peas

1 low-salt vegetable or chicken stock cube

2 x 250g packets of mixed precooked grains, which may include green lentils, pearl barley, quinoa, bulgar wheat (ensure no added salt)

30g (¾oz) Cheddar, grated, plus extra to serve

1 heaped tbsp mascarpone

freshly ground black pepper

garlic-infused olive oil, to serve (optional)

Heat the oil in a saucepan over a low-medium heat, add the onion and sauté for 2 minutes, stirring often so the edges don't catch. Add the garlic and cook for another 2 minutes.

Add the frozen peas and 300ml (10fl oz) of boiling water. Crumble in the stock cube and add a good grinding of black pepper. Stir and let it all simmer for 6 minutes until the peas are cooked.

Place the pan on a board, off the heat. Then, using a hand-held blender, purée the mixture well. Stir in the mixed grains and add another 100–150ml (3½–5fl oz) of water depending on the consistency – you want it to be a thick, dropping consistency. Return to the heat to cook for 5 minutes until bubbling, then spoon in the mascarpone and grated cheese – it will turn really creamy.

Serve with an extra grating of cheese and an optional little drizzle of garlic-infused olive oil. You can serve this as it is to the whole family from 6 months of age, however, if you wish, you can blend baby's portion down so it's smoother for them.

This will keep for a couple of days in the fridge or freeze for up to 3 months. Turn left overs into crisp cheesy surprise arancini balls (see page 84).

WASTE NOT, WANT NOT!

Bought a tub of mascarpone for this recipe and not sure what to do with the leftovers? Try mixing with crushed berries and spooning over puff pastry before popping in the oven for 20 minutes for a delicious sugar-free breakfast pastry. Or upgrade your cheese toastie by spreading crumpets with mascarpone, topping with grated cheese and baking on high until the cheese is oozy and golden! Better still, try the cheese twists on page 113.

CHEESY SURPRISE ARANCINI BALLS

Crispy on the outside but soft and gooey in the middle... If you manage to have any tasty Gorgeous Grains Cheat's Risotto left over, then this is what you should do with it! What a way to turn leftovers into something you'll all be fighting over!

🍴 **8 balls**

⏱ **20 minutes**

400g (14oz) cold leftover gorgeous grains cheat's risotto (roughly half the recipe), see page 83

70g (2½oz) plain (all-purpose) flour

30g (¾oz) Cheddar, grated (or try using smoked Cheddar for an extra flavour hit)

1 egg

50–70g (1¾–2½oz) panko breadcrumbs

½ x 125g ball of mozzarella

½ tbsp sunflower, olive or groundnut oil

Preheat the oven to 200°C fan (220°C/425°F/Gas 7).

Measure the risotto into a bowl with the flour and Cheddar, and stir well to combine.

Beat the egg in one bowl and add the breadcrumbs to another bowl.

Slightly wet your hands with water, then take a golf ball-sized amount of the mixture and roll into a ball. Flatten the ball in the palm of your hand and place a small pinch of mozzarella in the centre. Fold over the edges and roll back into a ball. Place in the egg bowl and roll out another 2 balls.

Now coat the 3 balls in the egg, then in the breadcrumbs and place on a baking tray.

Wash your hands quickly, keeping your hands ever so slightly wet, then repeat with the remaining mixture.

Drizzle each ball with a little oil, then pop in the preheated oven for 15–20 minutes until the breadcrumbs have turned golden. Serve warm with some yogurt or tomato sauce for dipping.

You can use this recipe for any leftover risotto you have.

TOP TIP!

Depending on your original risotto recipe, you may not need all of the flour (if you can easily form the rice into a ball and it's not too sticky, omit the flour all together).

QUICK LENTIL DAHL

Packed full of the good stuff, mildly spiced but bursting with tongue-tingling flavour, this dahl will spice up your midweek dinners for sure!

🍴 **2 adults and 2 littles**
⏱ **15 minutes**

1 tbsp garlic-infused olive oil
1 onion, coarsely grated
1 tbsp tomato purée (paste)
2 large garlic cloves, finely grated
2.5cm (1in) piece of ginger, peeled and finely grated
2 tsp smoked paprika
1 tsp ground turmeric
1 tsp ground coriander
2 tsp mild garam masala
½ tsp ground cumin
2 x 380g packets of cooked lentils in water (no added salt)
130g (4½oz) frozen chopped spinach (about 6 blocks)
freshly ground black pepper

TO SERVE
4 eggs (optional*)
small bunch of coriander (cilantro)
1 tbsp sesame seeds

Heat the garlic-infused olive oil in a saucepan, add the grated onion and sauté for about 2–3 minutes, stirring often, until the onion has turned translucent.

Once the onion has softened, add the tomato purée, garlic and ginger, along with the spices. Cook for a minute, stirring often to ensure nothing burns.

Now add the lentils, including the water from the packets, plus the frozen spinach. Give it all a good stir, and bring the dahl to the boil. Put the lid on, lower the heat and let it simmer for 10 minutes, stirring 2–3 times to help break up the spinach and ensure it's not sticking to the bottom of the pan.

While the dahl cooks, bring a separate pan of water to boil. Add the eggs and set a timer for 8 minutes. (Tip: To stop your eggs cracking when boiling, use an egg pricker, or a sharp needle to prick the round edge of the egg, this lets steam escape stopping the shell bursting.) Once cooked, drain away the hot water and cover the eggs with cold. Set aside until the dahl is ready.

Serve the dahl with a sprinkling of coriander, a halved boiled egg and a scattering of sesame seeds. Boiled rice or flatbreads (see page 44) work well on the side.

You can serve the dahl as is to baby, as none of the lumps are too big, but equally you can mash or blend, if you prefer.

This dahl will keep in the fridge for 2 days or the freezer for up to 4 months.

LENTIL SWAPS!
Using ready-cooked lentils makes this cheat's lentil dahl very quick and easy to whip together. However, you can also use 200g (7oz) of dried yellow lentils with 2 x 400ml cans coconut milk, and let the dahl simmer away for 40–60 minutes, which will intensify the flavours even more.

MY FIRST CURRY

Mild coconut, pea and chicken curry. Ready in just 15 minutes, this
flavourful meal is a great way to introduce Indian flavours to baby.

GF

EF

DF

🍴 2 adults and 2 littles
⏱ 15 minutes

1 mug of basmati rice
1 tbsp coconut or
   sunflower oil
6 skinless, boneless
   chicken thighs, or
   3 large chicken breasts,
   cut into 2cm (¾in)
   wide strips
1½ tbsp tomato purée
   (paste)
2 garlic cloves, crushed
1 tsp ground turmeric
2 tsp mild curry powder
1 tsp ground cumin
1½ tsp garam masala
1 tsp paprika
1 tsp mango powder
   (optional)
400ml can coconut milk
2 big handfuls of frozen
   peas
freshly ground black
   pepper

Pour the mug of rice into a saucepan. Fill the same mug up twice with boiling water from the kettle and add to the rice. Place the saucepan over a high heat and bring it to the boil, then put the lid on, reduce the heat to a simmer and cook for 12 minutes. Don't take the lid off until the time is up.

Meanwhile, in a separate saucepan, melt the coconut oil over a medium heat, add the chicken strips and cook for 4 minutes, stirring every so often.

Add the tomato purée, garlic, all of the spices and a good grinding of black pepper, and cook for 30–60 seconds, stirring constantly so they don't burn.

Add the coconut milk and frozen peas. Half-fill the empty coconut can with cold water, swilling the liquid around to gather as much of the coconut milk into the water as possible, then add this to the curry. Stir and let it all bubble away for around 8 minutes until the rice is done. Add more water if you feel the sauce is becoming too thick.

Once the rice timer is up, turn off the heat and remove the lid. Use a fork to move one section of rice away gently so you can see the bottom of the pan. If you see no water at the base of the pan and the rice looks fluffy, it's done. Place the lid back on the rice and let it rest for 2 minutes or until you're ready to serve.

Fluff the rice up with a fork and serve alongside the curry.

This curry is great to serve baby as a finger food. Or you can blitz up a small amount along with some rice and serve as a purée for baby, or chop the chicken and mix through the rice for a more textured meal. Another tip is to mix a little rice with some of the curry sauce and roll into a ball. This helps baby pick up the rice and eat it independently.

ADD SOME SPICE!
Don't shy away from introducing spice to baby from the age of 6 months. Getting your little one used to a variety of flavours is important for raising a confident eater. If you like stronger heat, add a scattering of fresh chilli or dried chilli flakes to adult plates.

CHICKEN FRIED RICE

DF

Inspired by the Indonesian rice dish Nasi Goreng, this flavourful chicken fried rice is super easy to whip together. It is really soft and easy to clump together in little balls, so baby can feed themselves, or alternatively chop up the chicken to spoon feed baby.

🍴 **2 adults and 2 littles**
⏱ **15 minutes**

1½ tbsp garlic-infused olive oil

3 skinless chicken breasts, sliced into 1cm (½in) wide strips

2 banana shallots, halved and thinly sliced

1 tbsp tomato purée (paste)

2 large garlic cloves, finely grated

2cm (¾in) piece of ginger, peeled and finely grated

2 x 250g packets of cooked basmati rice, squeezed to separate the grains

3 tbsp low-salt soy sauce

juice of 1 lime

2 eggs, beaten

freshly ground black pepper

TO SERVE

2 spring onions (scallions), thinly sliced

½ cucumber, cut into wedges

3 salad tomatoes, cut into wedges

Heat 1 tbsp of the garlic-infused olive oil in a large non-stick frying pan over a medium-high heat. Add the chicken and let it sit for a minute, then flip to cook the other side, and fry for another 3 minutes, stirring often until the chicken has just cooked. Remove from the pan and set aside.

Once the chicken is cooked, put the pan back on the heat, and reduce to medium. Add the remaining ½ tbsp garlic-infused olive oil and the sliced shallots. Cook for 1–2 minutes, stirring often so they don't catch, then add the tomato purée, garlic and ginger, and cook for a further minute, stirring often so they don't burn. Add the packet rice, soy sauce and lime juice. Cook for around 4 minutes, or until the rice has warmed up and is well coated in all the flavours, stirring every so often to help it along.

Add the chicken to the rice, including any resting juices, stir, then make a well in the centre so you can see the bottom of the pan. Pour in the beaten egg, then gently start to incorporate the rice into the egg, stirring well so every grain of rice is covered. It will take only a couple of minutes for the egg to cook and then it's ready to serve. Season with black pepper to taste.

Serve with a sprinkling of sliced spring onion on top, and fresh tomato and cucumber wedges on the side. Adults, you may want to add an extra splash of soy sauce to your plate.

You can either leave the chicken in strips and let baby eat with their fingers, or transfer baby's chicken portion to a chopping board and rock a sharp knife over it to cut it into small pieces, then mix in with the rice to spoon feed to baby.

To store leftovers, spread them over a large, cold plate in a thin, even layer. You must cool down cooked rice within an hour for it to be safe enough to keep. Store in the fridge for 24 hours or in the freezer for 3 months. Once defrosted, put back in a hot frying pan with an extra splash of water. Heat until piping hot before cooling and serving.

MAKE IT JUICY!
Juicing a lime can be quite difficult.
Before you slice it in half, roll the lime
on a work surface with the palm of your
hand as hard as you can. This will soften
the fruit, making it much easier to juice.

BABY-FRIENDLY CHILLI CON CARNE

EF

DF*

Kidney beans are high in protein and fibre, but their shape isn't ideal for babies. Try mashing them before adding – it helps thicken the sauce and makes them safer for babies to explore. This recipe is also great for batch cooking!

🍴 **2 adults and 2 littles**
⏱ **25 minutes**

2 tsp sunflower oil
1 onion, finely diced
500g (1lb 2oz) lean minced
    (ground) beef
1 heaped tbsp tomato purée
    (paste)
1 heaped tsp mixed dried herbs
½ tsp ground cumin
1 tsp Worcestershire sauce

1 heaped tsp smoked paprika
1 low-salt beef stock cube
400g can chopped tomatoes
400g can kidney beans in water
    (ensure no added salt)
20g (¾oz) dark (bittersweet)
    chocolate (optional)
freshly ground black pepper

Heat the oil in a large pan over a medium heat. Add the onion and cook, stirring, until translucent. Add the beef and tomato purée. Cook for 4–5 minutes, breaking up the meat with a wooden spoon.

Add the mixed dried herbs, cumin, Worcestershire sauce, smoked paprika and a good grinding of black pepper, and crumble in the stock cube. Give it a good stir, then add the canned tomatoes. Fill the tomato can one-third of the way up with water and swill out any of the tomato juice into the pan. Stir, cover and bring back to a simmer.

Meanwhile, drain and rinse the kidney beans and place in a large bowl. Using a potato masher, mash the beans until you have a rough paste, a few lumps are totally fine, you just don't want any whole kidney beans. Little hands can help with this!

Roughly chop the chocolate (if using) and add to the pan along with the kidney bean paste, then stir through. Cover and simmer for 15 minutes, topping it up with water if it becomes too dry.

Serve with rice, avocado and sour cream (unless dairy free*).

BABY-FRIENDLY LAMB KEBABS

*Lamb can sometimes be a little tough to chew, so using minced lamb makes
the meat much more succulent and soft, so it's easier and safer for baby to
have a good go at digging in.*

EF

DF*

🍴 10 small kebabs
⏱ 20 minutes

500g (1lb 2oz) 15–20%
    fat minced (ground)
    lamb
2 garlic cloves, crushed
2 heaped tbsp finely
    chopped chives
4 tsp smoked paprika
finely grated zest and
    juice of 1 lemon
2 heaped tsp plain
    (all-purpose) flour
freshly ground black
    pepper
baking tray, lined with
    non-stick baking paper

CUCUMBER PICKLE

1 cucumber, peeled and
    cut into 7.5cm (3in)
    matchsticks
1 tbsp white wine vinegar
juice of ½ lemon
½ garlic clove, crushed
freshly ground black
    pepper

Preheat the oven to 220°C fan (240°C/475°F/Gas 9).

Add all the kebab ingredients to a bowl and give it a good stir
and smush using your hands. You want all the ingredients to mix
well into the meat. Take slightly larger than golf ball amounts of
the meat and roll into a ball in the palm of your hands. Slightly
elongate the ball into a rough fat sausage shape, then roll either
end to a point.

Place on a lined baking tray and bake for 15–20 minutes until
golden and cooked all the way through.

While the kebabs cook, mix the cucumber pickle ingredients
together, cover and set aside for at least 15 minutes. This pickle
will last in the fridge for 5 days, but will start to soften over time.

Allow the kebabs to cool slightly and cut into quarters lengthways
before serving to the little ones. Serve the kebabs with a good
wedge of lemon, quick flatbreads (see page 44), the cucumber
pickle, my garlic and lemon "dip-dip" (see page 154) or yogurt of
your choice* and a picky salad.

These kebabs will store in the fridge for 2 days or freeze for up
to 2 months.

ADD SOME CRUNCH!
This stir-fry isn't as
crunchy as traditional
recipes. Adults can add
toasted cashews to
their plates for texture.

MY FIRST STIR-FRY

This method of flash-cooking the beef ensures it's really soft and tender, flaking away easily for baby to eat. The trick is to not over-cook it!

EF

DF

🍴 1 adults and 2 littles
⏱ 15 minutes

3 large broccoli florets, cut into smaller, long, bite-sized pieces
1 red (bell) pepper, cut into thin strips
⅓ low-salt beef stock cube (wrap the rest back up and save for another day)
1 level tsp cornflour (cornstarch)
2 tbsp low-salt soy sauce

1 tsp rice wine vinegar or white wine vinegar
1 tsp sesame oil
250g (9oz) sirloin steak
2 tsp stir-fry oil or garlic-infused olive oil
2 garlic cloves, finely grated
2cm (¾in) piece of ginger, finely grated

Bring a pan of water to the boil and add the broccoli. After 3 minutes, add the thinly sliced peppers and blanch for a further 2 minutes. Drain and set aside.

Crumble the stock cube into a jug and add 100ml (3½fl oz) of boiling water from the kettle. Add the cornflour, soy sauce, rice wine vinegar and sesame oil, stir well and set aside.

Remove the fat and any gristle from the steak and cut into 1cm (½in) strips. You can ask your butcher to do this bit.

Heat a large frying pan or wok over a high heat, then add 1 tsp of the stir-fry oil, the beef, garlic and ginger. Stir-fry for 1–2 minutes until just under-cooked. Remove from the pan and set aside.

Add the remaining oil to the hot pan, then fry the blanched veg for 3–4 minutes to finish cooking them and gain a little colour.

Add the sauce and meat, and cook for a further couple of minutes until the sauce has thickened and the beef is cooked through. Serve immediately (with boiled rice or noodles) to ensure the beef doesn't carry on cooking in the pan, which would make it turn tough and chewy.

COCONUT, CORN AND FISH CHOWDER

Creamy coconut milk soup, packed with sweetcorn, soft potato and flaky fish. This is a one-pot wonder of flavourful nutrition.

🍴 2 adults and 2 littles
⏲ 30 minutes

20g (½oz) unsalted butter or oil of your choice*

1 onion, finely diced

300g (10oz) potatoes (about 2 medium potatoes), peeled and cut into 1.5cm (½in) chunks

400g can coconut milk

100ml (3½fl oz) milk of your choice*

150g (5½oz) frozen or canned sweetcorn

400g (14oz) mixed boneless fish (a bag of fish pie mix works well, which includes smoked and unsmoked fish chunks)

3 slices of streaky (fatty) bacon (optional)

freshly ground black pepper

1 tbsp finely chopped chives, to serve (optional)

Heat the butter in a large, high-sided frying pan with a lid, but with the lid off for now. Add the onion and sauté over a medium-high heat for 4 minutes, stirring often until the onion has turned translucent.

Once the onion has softened, add the potato and cook for a further 2 minutes. Add the coconut milk, then pour the 100ml (3½fl oz) of milk into the empty can, swilling it around to gather up as much of the coconut milk as you can. Add to the pan along with the sweetcorn and a good grinding of black pepper, then put the lid on and simmer for 10 minutes.

Once the potato has softened, remove the pan from the heat and, using a hand-held blender, blitz until fairly smooth but with a few chunks of potato still intact.

Put the pan back on the heat and add the fish, stirring a little to ensure the pieces are evenly distributed. Put the lid back on the pan and cook for 8-10 minutes until the fish is cooked all the way through and flakes away easily.

Meanwhile, finely slice the bacon, and add to a separate hot frying pan. Cook for 5 minutes or until crispy. Once cooked, transfer to a bowl lined with kitchen paper to catch the excess fat.

Serve the chowder sprinkled with the chopped chives and crispy bacon pieces. If serving to baby, mash any larger pieces of potato with the back of a fork, don't worry about the fish as it flakes away really easily. You can also completely mash or blend the chowder to spoon feed to baby.

NUTRITION NOTE
There is no real risk in serving bacon to baby, and it's really great to offer a wide variety of tastes and textures. However the salt content is higher than other ingredients, so keep their sprinkles to a tiny taste.

SPINACH AND CHICKEN OPEN TOP TART

Flaky pastry, herby tomato sauce, thin slices of chicken, nutritious spinach and oozy melted cheese. Such a winning combo for lunch or dinner, and ideal for lunch boxes or eating on the go.

🍴 3 adults and 2 littles

⏲ 20 minutes

375g pack of ready-rolled puff pastry

100g (3½oz) frozen chopped spinach (about 5 blocks), see below

2 chicken breasts, thinly sliced

120g (4oz) Cheddar or mozzarella, grated

freshly ground black pepper

SAUCE

3 tbsp tomato purée (paste)

1 tsp garlic-infused olive oil

1 tsp mixed dried herbs

1 tsp smoked paprika

6 tbsp cold water

freshly ground black pepper

Preheat the oven to 200°C fan (220°C/425°F/Gas 7) and take the pastry out of the fridge to come up to room temperature a little.

Place the spinach in a microwaveable bowl, add a splash of water, cover and microwave for 2–3 minutes until the spinach has just defrosted.

Meanwhile, unroll the pastry and place onto a non-stick baking tray. Mix all the sauce ingredients together in a small bowl, then spread evenly over the pastry leaving a 1cm (½in) gap around the edge.

Scatter the sliced chicken evenly over the tomato sauce.

Squeeze out as much excess moisture as you can from the spinach using your hands (or a spoon if it's too hot), then separate the leaves and distribute evenly across the tart. Top with the cheese and a grinding of black pepper.

Bake in the preheated oven for 15 minutes until the pastry has puffed up, the chicken is cooked and the cheese is melted and golden. Cut into finger-sized strips to serve to baby.

The tart will keep in the fridge for 2 days, or freeze for up to 3 months. To reheat, defrost thoroughly and place in a hot oven for 10–13 minutes, or until completely piping hot.

SPINACH SWAP!

To use fresh spinach instead of frozen, put 2 large handfuls of baby leaf spinach into a colander over the sink. Pour over boiling water from the kettle until the spinach has wilted. Pop between a couple of sheets of kitchen paper to drain the excess water.

SPINACH AND RICOTTA PUFF PARCELS

V

Crispy, flaky pastry, soft and creamy ricotta and vitamin-rich spinach! These melt-in-the-mouth pastries make a fantastic lunch or dinner. They are delicious cold too, making them a good option for feeding the little one when out and about.

8 parcels
20 minutes

375g pack of ready-rolled
    puff pastry
100g (3½oz) frozen
    chopped spinach
    (about 5 blocks)
200g (7oz) ricotta
100g (3½oz) Cheddar,
    grated
2 eggs
freshly ground black
    pepper

Preheat the oven to 200°C fan (220°C/425°F/Gas 7) and take the pastry out of the fridge to come up to room temperature a little.

Defrost the spinach in the microwave for 1–2 minutes until just defrosted, but not warm. Then, using a fork, squeeze out as much moisture as you can, transferring the squeezed spinach into a separate bowl, discarding the liquid. Add the ricotta, some black pepper, half the grated cheese and 1 of the eggs, then mix together using a fork.

Unroll the pastry, cut it into 8 squares and lay them on a large non-stick baking tray. Spoon 2 tbsp of the ricotta mixture onto each pastry square in a diagonal fashion, leaving the corners bare. Cover the mixture with the remaining grated cheese.

Whisk the remaining egg and, using a pastry brush, apply egg wash on all the exposed pastry, paying attention to the corners. Tightly fold over the two opposite corners of pastry so they layer over each other, and the egg wash seals the pastry together.

Egg wash the tops of the parcels, and bake in the preheated oven for 15 minutes, or until puffed up and golden on top. Cut into strips to serve to baby so they can pick it up and eat it easily on their own. Enjoy hot or cold.

These parcels will keep in the fridge for 2 days. To reheat, place back in the oven for 5 minutes or until piping hot inside. You can also freeze them for up to 3 months. Place in the oven at 200°C fan (220°C/425°F/Gas 7) from frozen and cook for 10–15 minutes, or until defrosted and piping hot inside.

SHAPE SWAP!
Try making this recipe in a pinwheel style by spreading the ingredients over the sheet of pastry, rolling up, cutting into discs and baking for the same amount of time.

Fussy Eaters

HEALTHY "JUICE"

*As you start to wean baby, it is advised to offer them a drink of water in
a cup with their meals. Up until they're one, babies don't need additional
water for hydration, but it's good practice to get them used to using a cup.
As they enter those fiercely independent toddler years, sometimes it can
be difficult to get them to drink enough water. Try adding a touch of extra
flavour and calling it "juice" to get them interested. I won't tell, if you don't!*

⁐ 2 adults and 2 littles
⏱ 5 minutes

BLACKBERRY AND LEMON JUICE

handful of blackberries
(fresh or frozen and
defrosted)
juice of 1 lemon

In a bowl, mash the blackberries with the back of a fork, and add
the juice of a lemon. Add the pulp to a fine sieve (strainer) and,
using the back of a spoon, push the fruit through the sieve into a
jug (pitcher) containing 1.2 litres (2 pints) of water. Stir and serve.

RASPBERRY AND MINT JUICE

small sprig of mint
handful of raspberries
(fresh or frozen and
defrosted)

Crush and roll the mint in your hand to release the oils, then add
to a jug (pitcher) containing 1.2 litres (2 pints) of water. Put the
raspberries in a fine sieve (strainer) and push the fruit through
using the back of a spoon into the jug of water. Stir and let it
infuse in the fridge for 10 minutes. Remove the sprig and serve.

ORANGE AND STRAWBERRY JUICE

handful of strawberries
(fresh or defrosted)
juice of 1 orange

In a bowl, mash the strawberries with the back of a fork. Add
the juice of the orange, then, using the back of a spoon, push this
pulp through a fine sieve (strainer) into a jug (pitcher) containing
1.2 litres (2 pints) of water. Stir and serve.

CUCUMBER AND BLUEBERRY JUICE

7.5cm (3in) piece of
cucumber
handful of blueberries
(fresh or frozen and
defrosted)

In a pestle and mortar, pound the cucumber until you have a
thick, lumpy paste. Add the blueberries and crush too. Spoon this
pulp into a fine sieve (strainer) and scrape the juice into a jug
(pitcher) containing 1.2 litres (2 pints) of water. Stir and serve.

CARROT CAKE PORRIDGE

Just imagine, cake for breakfast! Ready in only 5 minutes, this porridge seriously tastes like carrot cake, without any of the guilt!!

🍴 **1 adult and 2 littles**
⏱ **5 minutes**

3 carrots, finely grated
1 mug rolled (old-fashioned) porridge oats
2 mugs milk of your choice*
2 tsp ground cinnamon
½ tbsp maple syrup (optional)

Add the grated carrots and oats to a saucepan and place over a medium heat. Then use the same mug to measure out the 2 mugs of milk, so you have a 2:1 ratio of milk to oats.

Add the cinnamon and syrup (if using), and cook for 4-5 minutes stirring constantly until thickened to your desired consistency.

If you have an impatient hungry little one wanting to be fed straight away, serve the porridge on a plate rather than a bowl – this way it'll cool much quicker.

Left over porridge will last for 2 days in the fridge or up to 3 months in the freezer. Reheat with an extra splash of milk until piping hot.

TOP TIPS

The size of mug you use doesn't matter, however the larger the mug the more porridge you'll get. One standard builder's mug will feed 1 adult and 2 littles.

Switch up the carrot for grated apple with a small handful of raisins for apple pie porridge.

SPINACH AND SWEETCORN MUFFINS

Soft, savoury muffins, packed full of vitamin-rich spinach with a delicious sweetness coming from the corn. A great recipe to batch cook and freeze – these muffins will defrost in a few hours, which makes them perfect to pack up for weaning on the go.

🍴 12 muffins
⏱ 25 minutes

160g (5½oz) frozen
   chopped spinach
   (7–8 blocks)
125g (4oz) unsalted
   butter or coconut oil*,
   melted
180g (6oz) self-raising
   (self-rising) flour
60ml (2fl oz) milk of your
   choice*
200g (7oz) drained
   canned sweetcorn
   (ensure no added salt)
4 eggs or 4 chia eggs,
   see page 140*
1 tsp baking powder
100g (3½oz) grated
   Cheddar or 2 tbsp
   nutritional yeast
   (optional)*
non-stick 12-hole muffin
   tin, greased

Preheat the oven to 180°C fan (200°C/400°F/Gas 6).

Add the frozen spinach to a bowl with a tiny drizzle of water, cover and defrost in the microwave until the ice has melted, but try not to cook the spinach. This should take around 90–180 seconds. Then squeeze out as much liquid as possible.

Add the spinach, along with the rest of the ingredients, to a mixing bowl and stir until combined, making sure to avoid over-mixing.

Spoon into the prepared muffin tin and bake in the preheated oven for 20 minutes until puffed up and cooked through.

Store in an air-tight container at room temperature for 3 days, or freeze for up to 3 months. To quickly defrost, blast on high in the microwave for 2–3 minutes, moving halfway through. Ensure they are piping hot, before cooling and serving. You can also defrost at room temperature, and serve cold if desired.

MINI VEG EGGY BITES

These soft and pillowy egg bites are packed full of veg! A tasty and easy way to add in some extra veggies any time of the day!

⏀ 24 bites
⏱ 25 minutes

1 small red (bell) pepper
1 small yellow (bell)
   pepper
4 chestnut (cremini)
   mushrooms
3 florets of broccoli
1 tsp garlic-infused olive
   oil
6 eggs
50g (1¾oz) Cheddar,
   grated (optional*)
freshly ground black
   pepper
24-hole silicone mini
   muffin mould, greased

Chop the peppers and mushrooms into 1cm (½in) cubes. Run the point of a knife around the stem of the broccoli florets to remove the stalk, and roughly chop the broccoli pieces to the same size as the peppers and mushrooms.

Preheat the oven to 180°C fan (200°C/400°F/Gas 6) and get a large non-stick frying pan on the hob to heat up.

Add all the veg to the frying pan along with the garlic-infused olive oil, and sauté for 5–10 minutes until the veg has softened.

Meanwhile, crack the eggs into a jug (pitcher), add the cheese and whisk until the egg white has combined well into the yolk.

Divide the veg mixture between the 24 holes of the mini muffin mould. Pour in the egg mixture and bake in the preheated oven for 15 minutes until the egg has puffed up and gained a lovely golden colour.

These will keep for 2 days in the fridge, or freeze for up to 3 months. Reheat in the microwave or pop in the oven until piping hot inside.

TOP TIP
You can use a regular 12-hole muffin tin by adding an extra 5–10 minutes onto the baking time.

CHEESE AND CHIVE SCONES

It's so quick and easy to whip up a batch of these cheesy, chive-spiked savoury scones. Try this upgraded British classic for a quick, fuss-free lunch, or play date snacks that the mums and dads will want to join in on!

EF

V

🍴 **7 scones**

⏱ **15 minutes**

200g (7oz) self-raising (self-rising) flour

50g (1¾oz) cold unsalted butter, cut into cubes

40g (1½oz) Cheddar, grated

1 tbsp finely chopped chives

130ml (4½fl oz) full-fat (whole) milk

Preheat the oven to 200°C fan (220°C/425°F/Gas 7).

Measure the flour and butter into a large bowl, then, using your fingertips, rub the butter into the flour until it resembles fine breadcrumbs. (Tip: If you shake the bowl gently, any large pieces of butter which haven't been rubbed into the flour yet will rise to the surface.)

Stir in the cheese and chives, then pour in the milk. Using a dinner knife, quickly stir and cut the dough so it all combines. Be careful not to over-mix.

Once the dough has just started to come together, tip out onto a floured surface and quickly but gently knead together. Pat the dough into a rough circle 2cm (¾in) in thickness. Then using a 7cm (3in) cutter, cut out your scones. Lightly knead back together the rest of the dough to cut out as many scones as possible. Alternatively, pat the dough into a rough circle, then cut into wedges using a sharp knife.

Place the scones on a non-stick baking tray and lightly brush the tops with a little milk. Try not to let the milk drip down the sides of the scones as this prevents a high rise when baking.

Bake in the preheated oven for 12–15 minutes until puffed up and golden brown on top. Don't open the oven door before 10 minutes as this can cause the scones to sink.

SIMPLE SWAPS!
Fancy something a little different? Swap out the chives for a handful of fresh blueberries, to make blueberry and cheese scones. Don't knock it until you've tried it, there's something about this combo that just works!

CHEESE TWISTS

Cheesy and soft on the inside – and deliciously crispy and flaky on the outside. These won't stick around for long!

10 twists

20 minutes

375g pack of ready-rolled
   puff pastry
2 heaped tbsp
   mascarpone
70g (2½oz) cheese,
   grated
1 egg, beaten
freshly ground black
   pepper

Preheat the oven to 200°C fan (220°C/425°F/Gas 7) and take the pastry out of the fridge to come up to room temperature a little.

Unroll the pastry sheet, then evenly spread over the mascarpone, ensuring you reach edge to edge. Generously grind over some black pepper, and then sprinkle over the cheese.

Fold the pasty in half lengthways and press down lightly. Cut into strips around 2.5cm (1in) in thickness. Twist each pastry strip as much as you can, and place on a non-stick baking tray, trying to place each end flat on the tray. Then brush the exposed pastry with the beaten egg.

Bake in the preheated oven for 15–20 minutes until puffed up and golden.

These twists are most delicious served warm, but also pack up great for weaning on the go. They can be frozen for up to 3 months. Either freeze before they are baked, and then bake from frozen for 20–25 minutes, or freeze once baked and cooled, and bake in a hot oven for 5–10 minutes to defrost and reheat.

COURGETTE, AVO AND MUSHROOM FRIES

Crispy on the outside and super soft in the middle, this is a great way to make often-refused veggies, fun and enjoyable! Suitable from 6 months, these are ideal finger food for little hands.

🍴 2 adults and 2 littles
⏱ 20 minutes

1 large just-ripe avocado
1 courgette (zucchini)
3 large flat mushrooms
3 heaped tbsp plain
  (all-purpose) flour
3 large (US extra-large)
  eggs or use about
  140ml (4¾fl oz) milk of
  your choice*
200g (7oz) panko
  breadcrumbs
freshly ground black
  pepper
olive or coconut oil
  cooking spray

Preheat the oven to 200°C fan (220°C/425°F/Gas 7).

To prep the veg, remove the skin and stone of the avocado, then slice into 1.5cm (½in) wide wedges. Cut the courgette into roughly 6cm (2½in) lengths, and then take each round, cut in half lengthways, then each half into 3 wedges. Wipe the mushrooms with kitchen paper, or if they're really dirty peel off the skin; it should remove easily. Do not wash the mushrooms as they will soak up too much water. Remove the stump from each mushroom and cut into 1.5cm (½in) wide strips.

Set up a dredging station by gathering three large, flat-bottomed bowls. Add the flour to the first bowl and mix in a good grinding of black pepper. Whisk the eggs in the second bowl and add the breadcrumbs to the final bowl.

Coat each piece of veg first in the flour, then the egg and finally the breadcrumbs. Ensure at each stage the veg is well coated.

Place onto a non-stick baking tray and spray each piece with a squirt of cooking oil. Bake in the preheated oven for about 15–20 minutes until crispy and golden. Serve these with the garlic and lemon "dip-dip" on page 154 and some chopped up fruit, if you like.

Once baked, store in the fridge for 2 days or in the freezer for up to 3 months. Thoroughly defrost before reheating back in the oven for 10–15 minutes or until piping hot inside.

FRIDGE-RAID HIDDEN VEG PASTA SAUCE

If you have lots of odds and ends left in your fridge veg drawer, take 30 minutes to whip up a huge batch of my 8-veg pasta sauce. Fill up the freezer with individual portions to take out on days when you're stretched for time. Your little veg-dodger will love it!

enough for 15 little portions of pasta

30 minutes

1 tbsp olive oil

1 large onion, diced

1 leek

2 carrots, cut into 2mm (⅛in) slices

1 large parsnip, cut into 2mm (⅛in) slices

2 x 400g cans good-quality plum tomatoes

1 red (bell) pepper, roughly chopped

1 green (bell) pepper, roughly chopped

1 small head of broccoli

2 garlic cloves

1 very low-salt chicken or vegetable stock cube*

1 tsp mixed dried herbs

1 tsp sugar (optional, but helps to cut through the tomato acidity)

2 heaped tsp smoked paprika

150g (5oz) grated Cheddar or 3 tbsp nutritional yeast*, plus extra to serve (optional)

freshly ground black pepper

Get the kettle on to boil. Heat the oil in a very large pan, add the onion and sauté over a medium heat until translucent.

Meanwhile, run a knife down the centre of the leek, keeping the stalk together, then wash under a running tap, open-side down, so any mud runs out between the leaves. Thinly slice the leek then add to the pan. Add the sliced carrots and parsnips, too.

Add the canned tomatoes, then half-fill each can with boiling water from the kettle, and swill them out into the pan. Give it all a good stir. Add the peppers.

Remove the woody end of the broccoli, keeping most of the stalk attached, then roughly chop the florets and finely chop the stem as this takes longer to cook. Add it all to the pot.

Place the side of your knife over the garlic cloves, and gently press with the palm of your hand to crush the cloves slightly. This allows the skin to come away easily, then add the flesh to the pot. Crumble in the stock cube, add a good grinding of black pepper, the dried herbs, sugar and smoked paprika.

Give it all a good stir and top up with boiling water to just cover the veg. Put the lid on and let it bubble for 20 minutes until the veg has softened.

Once cooked, use a hand blender to whizz it all up until super smooth, then add the cheese and let it melt into the sauce.

Serve with freshly cooked pasta and an extra sprinkle of cheese on top. This sauce keeps really well in the freezer – store it in portions for up to 3 months.

SWITCH IT UP!

You can swap out any ingredients for whatever you have to hand. The quantities and exact veg aren't vital, you just want to be able to fill your pot with veg to bulk out the body of the sauce.

CREAMY COURGETTE AND CHICKEN PASTA

Succulent chicken pieces are cooked in a creamy courgette and cheese sauce.
Stir through pasta for a super-quick and tasty midweek meal, which even
the fussiest of veg-dodgers will enjoy.

2 adults and 2 littles
15 minutes

250g (9oz) dried pasta
250ml (9fl oz) full-fat
   (whole) milk
4 boneless, skinless
   chicken thighs, or 2
   small chicken breasts
1½ tsp olive oil
1 small courgette
   (zucchini), grated
1 garlic clove, crushed or
   finely grated
1 tbsp cornflour
   (cornstarch)
150g (5oz) Cheddar,
   grated, plus extra to
   serve (try smoked
   Cheddar for a tasty
   kick)
freshly ground black
   pepper

Bring a pan of water to the boil and add the pasta. Cook
according to the packet instructions. Put a separate non-stick
frying pan on the heat to start warming up.

Add the milk to a microwaveable jug and heat for 2 minutes
on high to take away the fridge coldness.

Cut the chicken into 1.5cm (½in) thick strips, and add to the
frying pan with the oil. Cook for around 3 minutes, stirring
halfway through.

Now add the grated courgette to the chicken and sauté for
a couple of minutes until you can see it has started to soften.
Season with a good grinding of black pepper and add the garlic.

Add the cornflour to the chicken and courgette mixture, and stir
for 30 seconds to let the flour cook out. Then pour in the milk
and cook for around 5 minutes, stirring frequently, until the sauce
has thickened. Add the cheese and let it melt into the sauce.

Your pasta should be cooked by now. Reserve a small amount
of the cooking water in a mug and drain the pasta. Add the pasta
to the sauce along with a little dash of the reserved water. Stir
together and serve with an extra grating of cheese on top.

NUTRITION NOTE
Remember to skip the salt in the pasta cooking water. Babies
under 12 months of age can have a maximum of 1g of salt per
day. So it's best to salt your own plate at the table, rather than
whilst cooking.

CAULIFLOWER CHEESE GNOCCHI BAKE

V*

Super-smooth cauliflower and cheese sauce loaded with gorgeous little gnocchi bites.

🍴 2 adults and 2 littles
⏱ 25 minutes

400ml (14oz) full-fat (whole) milk
1 low-salt chicken or vegetable stock cube*
260g (9oz) cauliflower, cut into florets
1 heaped tsp cornflour (cornstarch)
½ tsp English mustard (optional)
190g (7oz) Cheddar, grated
500g vacuum pack of gnocchi
freshly ground black pepper

Preheat the oven to 220°C fan (240°C/475°F/Gas 9).

Measure the milk into a microwaveable jug (pitcher), crumble in the stock cube and add the cauliflower and a good grinding of black pepper. Microwave on high for 5 minutes.

Once the cauliflower milk is cooked, add the cornflour and mustard, then, using a hand-held blender, whizz up until smooth. Stir in two-thirds of the cheese, then pour into a large ovenproof baking dish.

Tip the gnocchi into the sauce, stir well, then top with the remaining cheese and a good extra grinding of black pepper.

Bake for 20 minutes until bubbling and the cheese has turned golden.

To serve to children under 18 months, cut each gnocchi into quarters, or you can mash or blend the gnocchi into the sauce once baked.

Any leftovers will keep for 2 days in the fridge or 2 months in the freezer. Add a splash more milk before reheating in the oven until bubbling and piping hot.

LASAGNE ROLL-UPS

Use up leftover mince or veggie ragu for this delicious quick-and-easy take on a traditional lasagne. It can be prepped and baked in about 30 minutes, making it a fairly quick dinner for all the family.

⊠ 2 adults and 2 littles
⏱ 30 minutes

400ml (14fl oz) full-fat
(whole) milk
30g (1oz) unsalted butter
2 tbsp cornflour
(cornstarch)
150g (5½oz) Cheddar,
grated
250g (9oz) fresh lasagne
sheets
at least ½ quantity
cheat's beef ragu, see
page 71, or lentil spag
bol, see page 156*
freshly ground black
pepper

Preheat the oven to 200°C fan (220°C/425°F/Gas 7).

Heat the milk in the microwave on high for 3 minutes. Melt the butter in a saucepan. Add the cornflour and cook for a minute, stirring constantly. Now add the warm milk gradually, stirring constantly. Cook for a few minutes until the sauce has thickened to a dropping consistency. Take the sauce off the heat, add some black pepper and two-thirds of the grated cheese, and stir until the cheese has melted into the sauce. Set aside.

Grab an ovenproof dish that is as wide as your pasta sheets. Place one sheet of pasta on a chopping board, add 2–3 tbsp of the cold ragu and spread it across the pasta from edge to edge.

Roll up the pasta sheet so you have a long sausage swirl, and place in the ovenproof dish. Repeat until you have used up all the pasta, and the lasagne roll ups are sitting snug in the dish. If you have some leftover ragu, spread it over the top of the lasagne roll-ups, and then cover everything with an extremely generous amount of the cheese sauce. You may not need to use it all, depending on the size of your oven dish. Sprinkle with the remaining cheese.

Bake it in the oven for 15–20 minutes until everything is bubbling and the cheese has turned golden on top.

TIME-SAVING TIP

If you have any leftover cheese sauce, pour into an ice cube tray and, once cooled, freeze for up to 3 months. For days where you're pushed for time and your little one needs their dinner right away – add 3 cubes of cheese sauce to a bowl with a small handful of frozen peas and an extra splash of milk and microwave on high for 2–3 minutes. Stir through freshly cooked pasta with an extra grating of cheese on top.

CHEESY COURGETTE PIZZA

V

This has to be one of my favourite recipes ever! Prep your pizza base in just
15 minutes with only two ingredients – no kneading and no need to let the
dough rise. Simple! This is the ultimate tasty finger food from 6 months,
and can even be popped into packed lunches.

🍴 **2 x 18cm (7in) pizzas**
   (1 adult and 2 littles)
⏲ **15 minutes**

PIZZA DOUGH

8 heaped tbsp self-raising
   (self-rising) flour, plus
   extra if needed
4 heaped tbsp plain
   full-fat Greek-style
   yogurt
1 tsp baking powder

TOPPING

½ courgette (zucchini)
70g (2½oz) Cheddar,
   grated
2 heaped tbsp full-fat
   cream cheese

Preheat the oven to 220°C fan (240°C/475°F/Gas 9).

Coarsely grate the courgette using a box grater, then squeeze
the strands in your hands over the sink to release the juices.
Add the pulp to a bowl along with the grated cheese, then
separate the courgette using your fingers, mixing it well with
the cheese. Set aside while you make the dough.

You can get your little ones involved with making the dough.
It's a great messy and sensory play idea that will also help avoid
fussy eating with those little veg-dodgers. Add the flour to a large
bowl along with the yogurt and baking powder. Stir with the
spoon until it starts to come together, then tip the entire contents
onto a clean work surface, scraping out any yogurt left in the
bowl. Gently bring the dough together; add an extra sprinkling
of flour if the dough feels too sticky. Within a minute or so, the
dough should form into a ball. Cut in half to make two pizzas.

Take one ball of dough and dust with a little extra flour. Then,
using a rolling pin, roll the dough into a circular shape around
1cm (½in) thick, moving and rotating as you go so it doesn't stick
to the surface.

Lightly dust a non-stick baking tray with flour. Transfer the pizza
base to the baking tray and spoon over 1 tbsp of the cream
cheese, using the back of the spoon to spread the cheese evenly
over the base. Sprinkle over half the courgette and cheese mixture.

Repeat with the other ball of dough and the remaining toppings.
Pop both pizzas into the preheated oven and cook for about
10–15 minutes until the base has puffed up and the cheese is
golden and crispy.

COCONUT CRUMB FISH FINGERS

DF

Using coconut instead of breadcrumbs to coat these fingers adds a delicious texture and flavour, which pairs really well with fish.

🍴 2 adults and 2 littles
⏱ 20 minutes

500g (1lb 2oz) skinless sustainable flaky fish, such as salmon, cod or bass

3 heaped tbsp plain (all-purpose) flour

2 eggs, beaten

5 tbsp desiccated (dried unsweetened shredded) coconut

freshly ground black pepper

olive oil cooking spray

Preheat the oven to 180°C fan (200°C/400°F/Gas 6).

Slice the fish into strips about 3cm (1¼in) wide.

Set up a dredging station with three bowls. Put the flour and a little grinding of black pepper in the first bowl, the beaten eggs in the next, and the desiccated coconut in the third bowl.

One by one, dip the fish into the flour, then into the egg and finally into the coconut, ensuring at each stage the fish is well coated. (You can freeze the fish fingers at this point, if making a stash.)

Place onto a non-stick baking tray, spray each fish finger with a little cooking oil and bake in the preheated oven for 15–20 minutes until golden and cooked all the way through.

TOP TIP

When dredging the fish, keep one hand for only the wet ingredients (i.e., picking up the wet fish, and dipping in the egg) and the other hand for only the dry ingredients (the flour and coconut). This way your fingers don't become a clumpy mess and it all goes much smoother.

FAMILY-FRIENDLY FAJITAS

EF

Flavourful chicken, peppers and onions are grilled until soft and succulent.
Serve with tortilla wraps or homemade flatbreads (see page 44), sour cream
and my easy-to-whip-together smooth guacamole.

🍴 **2 adults and 2 littles**
⏲ **15 minutes**

3 tbsp olive oil
1 heaped tbsp smoked
    paprika
1 tsp ground coriander
½ tsp ground cumin
2 tsp garlic granules
juice of ½ lime
3 large chicken breasts,
    cut into 1cm (½in) wide
    strips
1 red onion, finely sliced
1 red (bell) pepper, finely
    sliced
1 yellow (bell) pepper,
    finely sliced
6 tortilla wraps
4 tbsp full-fat Greek-style
    yogurt
40g (1½oz) cheese,
    grated

GUACAMOLE

2 ripe small avocados, or
    1 large avocado, flesh
    removed
juice of ½ lime
1 salad tomato
small bunch of coriander
    (cilantro)
freshly ground black
    pepper

Preheat the oven to 180°C fan (200°C/400°F/Gas 6).

Mix the olive oil, spices, garlic and lime juice together in a large
bowl. Add the chicken strips, onion and peppers. Stir and set
aside while you make the guacamole.

Take the tortilla wraps and encase in a big sheet of kitchen foil.
Place on a tray and pop in the preheated oven for 15 minutes
or until you're ready to serve – this will warm up the wraps and
make them lovely and soft, and easier to roll around your filling.

Add all the guacamole ingredients to a blender, reserving a few
coriander leaves to garnish, and blend until smooth. Transfer to
a serving bowl and sprinkle with the reserved coriander leaves
and a little black pepper. Set aside until ready to serve.

Heat a large griddle or non-stick frying pan over maximum heat.
Once searing hot, add the marinated chicken and veg, spreading
it out so every piece is touching the base of the hot pan. Let it
cook for 3 minutes before using a spatula to stir and flip every
piece of chicken, onion and pepper. Cook for 5–8 minutes or until
the chicken is fully cooked and the onion and peppers have
softened. Ensure to keep moving everything around so it doesn't
catch. If your griddle pan is small, you may need to cook it in two
batches. To check the chicken is cooked, tear open a thick piece
of chicken – if you see any pink meat inside, it needs a little more
cooking, it should be white and stringy once done.

To serve to the big kids, make up wraps with a spoonful of yogurt
and guacamole in the centre. Top with the cooked chicken and
veg and a little sprinkling of cheese. Fold in the sides of the wrap,
then roll up so all the filling is enclosed. Cut in half and serve with
a little picky salad on the side and more dips to dunk.

To serve to baby, plate up the fajitas de-constructed. The chicken
and veg is already cut into strips. Cut a quarter of a wrap into
strips for baby to dip into the yogurt and guacamole.

BUTTER CHICKEN

Succulent chicken bites in a smooth fragrant sauce. Don't be put off by the list of ingredients; this curry is really easy to make and will be a total crowd-pleaser.

EF

🍴 2 adults and 2 littles
⏱ 20 minutes

MARINADE
500g (1lb 2oz) skinless, boneless chicken thighs, cut into chunks
150g (5oz) full-fat Greek-style yogurt
juice of 1 lemon
1 tsp ground cumin
1 tsp garam masala
1 tsp garlic granules
2 tsp smoked paprika

SAUCE
20g (¾oz) unsalted butter
1 tsp garlic-infused olive or sunflower oil
1 onion, finely diced
3 tbsp tomato purée (paste)
3 garlic cloves, grated
thumb-sized piece of ginger, peeled and grated (optional)
2 tsp garam masala
1 low-salt chicken stock cube
100g (3½oz) full-fat Greek-style yogurt or double (heavy) cream
baking tray, lined with non-stick baking paper

Preheat the oven to 220°C fan (240°C/475°F/Gas 9).

Mix all the marinade and chicken pieces together. To make ahead, you can cover the marinated chicken and store in the fridge for up to 12 hours, the flavour will intensify the longer you marinate it for.

Place the chicken on the lined baking tray and pop in the oven for 10–15 minutes until the chicken is cooked through and starting to catch around the edges.

Meanwhile, to make the sauce, melt the butter and oil in a medium saucepan. Add the finely diced onion and cook for 3–4 minutes until softened.

Now add the tomato purée, garlic, ginger and garam masala and cook for a further 2–3 minutes, stirring continuously so the tomato purée doesn't burn on the bottom of the pan.

Dissolve the chicken stock cube into 200ml (7fl oz) boiling water, then add to the pan. Stir, then add the yogurt or cream.

Let the sauce come to the boil, then turn the heat down and simmer for 5 minutes.

Once the chicken is done, add to the pan along with any cooking juices, stir and serve with rice or flatbreads (see page 44).

To serve to baby, cut any larger piece of chicken in half lengthways, or remove the chicken from the sauce and chop finely on a chopping board, then add back to the sauce and stir through for baby. You can also blend to a smooth purée if you would prefer.

Any leftovers will keep for 2 days in the fridge or for up to 2 months in the freezer.

Freezer
Stash

PAN-FRIED FRITTERS TWO WAYS

I have been serving these sweetcorn and spinach fritters to my Nina ever since she was 6 months old. Packed full of veg, they can be kept in the fridge for 2 days or frozen for up to 6 months. The perfect freezer stash saviour! Beetroot can often be one ingredient that is turned away by fussy eaters. However, these cheesy little bites are always a hit in our house.

EF*

V

Vg*

DF*

🍴 **25 fritters each**
⏱ **10 minutes**

SWEETCORN AND SPINACH FRITTERS

200g (7oz) drained canned sweetcorn
100g (3½oz) wilted spinach, drained (you can also use 4 cubes of frozen spinach, defrosted in the microwave)
100g (3½oz) self-raising (self-rising) flour
2 eggs or 2 tbsp chia seeds mixed with an extra 75ml (2½fl oz) milk*
70ml (2½fl oz) milk of your choice*
1 tsp baking powder
sunflower, olive or coconut oil, for frying

BEETROOT FRITTERS

100g (3½oz) self-raising (self-rising) flour
1 tsp baking powder
90ml (3fl oz) milk of your choice*
2 eggs or 2 tbsp ground flaxseeds (linseeds) mixed with an extra 75ml (2½fl oz) milk*
60g (2oz) Cheddar, grated (optional)*
3 vacuum-packed cooked beetroots (beets)
sunflower or olive oil, for frying

Add all the ingredients to a blender and whizz up until smooth.

Heat a large, heavy-bottomed, non-stick frying pan with a little drizzle of oil over a medium heat. Spoon tablespoons of the mixture into the pan and, using the back of the spoon, gently shape the fritter into a neat circle. You will probably need to cook these fritters in batches of around 5 or 6.

After a minute or so, you'll start to see little bubbles forming on top of the fritters. Use a thin, sturdy, rubber spatula to flip the fritter over quickly. If you can't easily get the spatula under the fritter, it's not ready to be flipped.

Cook for a further minute on the other side until there is no raw mixture visible. Set aside on a plate while you cook the rest. You may need to turn the heat down if the fritters are browning too quickly.

Cut into strips to serve to baby, with some Greek-style yogurt or hummus (see page 45) for dipping.

TIME-SAVING TIP!
These fritters are great for keeping in the freezer, see page 135 for advice.

SHORTCUT SHEET PAN FRITTERS TWO WAYS

EF*

DF*

Sometimes it's nice spending 10 minutes at the stove top making up a batch of fritters or pancakes. However, some days there just aren't enough minutes let alone hours in the day. Quickly whip up the fritter batter, pour into a lined baking tray and bake in the oven until puffed up and golden. Total fuss-free cooking, with no compromise on the flavour!

🍴 **10 small fritters each**
⏱ **20 minutes**

TUNA AND SWEETCORN FRITTERS

90g (3oz) self-raising (self-rising) flour
2 eggs or 2 tbsp ground flaxseeds (linseeds) mixed with 75ml (2½fl oz) water*
70ml (2½fl oz) milk of your choice*
145g can tuna in spring water, drained
1 tsp baking powder
200g (7oz) drained canned sweetcorn
60g (2oz) Cheddar, grated (optional)*
1 spring onion (scallion), finely sliced
freshly ground black pepper
baking tray, lined with non-stick baking paper

COURGETTE FRITTERS

1 courgette (zucchini), grated and the liquid squeezed out
2 egg or 2 tbsp ground flaxseeds (linseeds) mixed with 75ml (2½fl oz) water*
100g (3¼oz) self-raising (self-rising) flour
1 tsp baking powder
80g (2½oz) grated Cheddar or 1 tbsp nutritional yeast (optional)*
80ml (2½fl oz) milk of your choice*
baking tray, lined with non-stick baking paper

Preheat the oven to 180°C fan (200°C/400°F/Gas 6).

Add all the ingredients to a bowl and stir until combined. Pour the batter into the lined baking tray and spread out evenly to about 1cm (½in) in thickness. If your baking tray is too large, form the batter into a smaller bake, ensuring the thickness is correct.

Bake in the preheated oven for 15–20 minutes until puffed up and golden on top.

Using a pizza cutter, cut into squares (or finger strips if serving to baby). Serve with a picky salad and some full-fat Greek-style yogurt for dipping.

These fritters will keep in the fridge for 2 days, or top up your freezer stash for up to 2 months. Either defrost and warm up in the microwave or allow to defrost at room temperature and reheat in the oven for 5 minutes until piping hot inside.

QUINOA AND BLACK BEAN CUPS

Soft, smokey and nutritious, here iron-rich heroes, quinoa and black beans, are formed into little cups perfect for little hands!

🍴 **11–12 cups**
⏱ **15 minutes**

230g packet of black
   beans in water
250g packet of cooked
   quinoa
2 beaten eggs or 2 chia
   eggs, see page 140*
1 tsp garlic powder or
   1 garlic clove, crushed
2 tsp smoked paprika
50g (1¾oz) self-raising
   (self-rising) flour
1 tsp baking powder
50g (1¾oz) grated
   Cheddar or 2 tbsp
   nutritional yeast*
freshly ground black
   pepper
non-stick 12-hole muffin
   tin, greased

Preheat the oven to 200°C fan (220°C/425°F/Gas 7).

Drain and rinse the black beans, shaking off any excess water, then add to a large mixing bowl. Mash the beans slightly with a potato masher, then add the rest of the ingredients.

Thoroughly mix, and spoon into the muffin tin.

Bake in the preheated oven for 15 minutes until the mixture has set and turned slightly golden on top.

Let the cups sit for a couple of minutes before removing from the tin and serving. Cut into strips to serve to baby, with a little yogurt of your choice* or hummus (see page 45) for dipping.

These will keep in the fridge for 3 days, or in the freezer for up to 3 months. Defrost thoroughly and reheat in the microwave or oven until piping hot.

CHICKEN AND BROCCOLI NUGGETS

Succulent kid-friendly chicken nuggets, but packed full of extra greens for those veg-dodging little ones.

🍴 **20 nuggets**
⏱ **20 minutes**

100g (3½oz) broccoli
80g (3oz) Cheddar,
  roughly cubed
  (optional)*
320g (11oz) skinless,
  boneless chicken
  thighs (I use thighs as
  they are more
  succulent, but breast
  also works)
1 egg
1 heaped tbsp cornflour
  (cornstarch)
1 tsp smoked paprika
2 large garlic cloves,
  roughly chopped
50g (1¾oz) breadcrumbs
freshly ground black
  pepper
olive oil cooking spray
baking tray, lined with
  non-stick baking paper

Preheat the oven to 220°C fan (240°C/475°F/Gas 9).

Add the broccoli and cheese to a food processor and blitz until it resembles breadcrumbs. Now add the chicken, egg, cornflour, smoked paprika, garlic and a good grinding of black pepper. Blend until well combined and there are no large pieces of chicken left to incorporate.

Add the breadcrumbs to a bowl ready for rolling.

Take a heaped teaspoon of the mixture and roll into a small ball in the palm of your hands. Drop it into the breadcrumbs and flatten the ball into a small patty shape as you coat the outside of the nugget in breadcrumbs. Place onto the lined baking tray and repeat until all the chicken mixture has been shaped.

Wash your hands, then spray each nugget with a squirt of cooking oil. Pop in the oven for 15–17 minutes until the chicken has cooked through and the nuggets have gained a lovely golden colour.

Serve with steamed veg or a picky salad, and sweet potato and parsnip wedges (see page 81).

Left over cooked nuggets will last in the fridge for 2 days or ideally kept in the freezer for up to 3 months. Bake from frozen at 180°C fan (200°C/400°F/Gas 6) for 20 minutes, until piping hot inside.

CHEESY CHIVE PANCAKES

Soft and fluffy with a delicious savoury cheese flavour, these pancakes are great for breakfast, lunch, dinner and even snacks. Perfect for packing up to take with you on days out, too.

🍴 12 pancakes
⏱ 10 minutes

170g (6oz) self-raising (self-rising) flour
1 tsp baking powder
2 eggs or 2 chia eggs, see page 140*
155ml (5fl oz) full-fat (whole) milk or plant-based alternative
1 tbsp finely chopped chives
50g (1¾oz) Cheddar, grated
freshly ground black pepper
olive, sunflower or groundnut oil, for frying

Add all the ingredients to a large bowl with a little black pepper, and stir until just combined.

Heat a large non-stick frying pan over a medium heat with a little oil and, once hot, spoon tablespoons of the batter into the pan, using the spoon to gently tease the mixture into a circle shape.

After a minute or so, when the pancakes are starting to firm up, flip and cook on the other-side. Repeat until all the mixture is used up. You may need to lower the temperature if the pancakes are burning quickly.

Cut into strips and serve with full-fat Greek yogurt for dipping.

To freeze, place a layer of baking paper between each pancake. Either defrost at room temperature and reheat in the oven or pan, or blast in the microwave turning every 30 seconds until fully defrosted and piping hot inside.

SWEETCORN AND CHICKPEA PATTIES

Protein-rich canned chickpeas are a really handy ingredient to have in your store cupboard. There are lots of dishes you can make from them, such as hummus or curries, or try these patties.

🍴 16 patties
⏱ 10 minutes

240g (8½oz) canned chickpeas (drained weight)
260g (9oz) canned sweetcorn (drained weight)
1 tbsp groundnut oil
1 garlic clove, grated
90g (3oz) Cheddar, grated (optional)*
1 tbsp chopped parsley
2 beaten eggs or 2 chia eggs, see page 140*
3 heaped tbsp self-raising (self-rising) flour
1½ tsp smoked paprika
freshly ground black pepper

Add the chickpeas and sweetcorn to a large bowl and coarsely mash using a potato masher. You want all of the chickpeas to have popped and squished a little, but don't worry if it's not a smooth purée.

Now add the rest of the ingredients and mix until well combined.

Heat a large non-stick frying pan over a medium high heat with the groundnut oil. Fry heaped tablespoons of the batter, shaping roughly into circle shapes as you spoon it into the pan. (You may find using two spoons helpful; one to scoop and one to scrape off the other spoon into the pan.)

After a couple of minutes, once you can easily get a spatula under the patties, flip them. Once on the other side, press down with the back of the spatula on top of each patty to slightly flatten it, ensuring it cooks through evenly.

Serve these patties, cut into strips for baby to dunk into yogurt, with a salad or as a veggie burger in buns.

Left over cooked patties will last in the fridge for 2 days or can be kept in the freezer for up to 3 months. Bake from frozen at 180°C fan (200°C/400°F/Gas 6) for 20 minutes, until piping hot inside.

BLEND IT UP!
If you would prefer a smoother textured patty, you can turn this recipe into little fritters by adding all the ingredients to a blender and whizzing up until smooth before frying. Remember, it's good to offer a variety of textures to baby so they become accustomed to a diverse diet.

SAVOURY FLAPJACK

A tasty and nutritious savoury take on the classic flapjack. A great finger food for baby, and an easy way to sneak in some veg for those fussy toddlers.

GF

EF*

V

Vg*

DF*

🍴 **12 flapjacks**
⏱ **25 minutes**

2 carrots
1 courgette (zucchini)
140g (5oz) Cheddar or
   2–3 tbsp nutritional
   yeast*
200g (7oz) rolled
   (old-fashioned)
   porridge oats
3 tsp chia seeds
   (optional)
3 tsp ground flaxseeds
   (linseeds) (optional)
100g (3½oz) unsalted
   butter or coconut oil,
   melted*
3 eggs or 3 chia eggs, see
   below*
1 tsp smoked paprika
20cm (8in) square baking
   tin, greased and lined
   with baking paper

Preheat the oven to 180°C fan (200°C/400°F/Gas 6).

Using a box grater, coarsely grate the carrots, courgette and cheese, then and add to a large bowl along with the rest of the ingredients.

Mix everything together until thoroughly combined, and tip the mixture into your prepared baking tin.

Press into all the corners using the back of a spoon, ensuring the mixture is flat and even.

Bake in the preheated oven for 20–25 minutes until the top is golden and crispy. Leave to cool in the tin for 5 minutes before transferring to a board and cutting into finger shapes with a serrated knife.

Once cold, pop half of the flapjacks in the freezer for up to 3 months to pull out on days when time is short. They can be eaten cold, once defrosted or, to reheat, cook straight from frozen in the microwave for 60-90 seconds or until piping hot, turning halfway through.

TRY CHIA EGG!
To make a chia egg substitute for hens' eggs, mix 1 tbsp chia seeds with 2½ tbsp warm water per 1 egg required, so for 2 eggs, use 2 tbsp chia seeds and 5 tbsp warm water, for 3 eggs use 3 tbsp chia seeds and 115ml (3½fl oz) warm water. Set the chia egg mixture aside for 10 minutes before using.

CHEESY CORNBREAD MUFFINS

V

These sweet and cheesy little muffins are packed full of vitamin C-rich corn.
The perfect little muffin to whip up to accompany any meal.

🍴 **12 muffins**
⏱ **20 minutes**

280g (10oz) canned
   sweetcorn (drained
   weight)
250g (9oz) fine cornmeal
150g (5½oz) self-raising
   (self-rising) flour
2 tsp baking powder
70g (2½oz) unsalted
   butter, melted
3 eggs
80g (3oz) full-fat
   Greek-style or natural
   (plain) yogurt
120g (4oz) Cheddar,
   grated
100ml (3½fl oz) full-fat
   (whole) milk or a
   plant-based alternative
12-hole muffin tin, lined
   with paper cases

Preheat the oven to 180°C fan (200°C/400°F/Gas 6).

Add all the ingredients to a blender, reserving 20g (¾oz) of the grated cheese, and blend until smooth.

Spoon the mixture into each case of the lined muffin tin.

Sprinkle with the reserved cheese then bake in the preheated oven for 15–20 minutes until puffed up and golden on top. To check the muffins are cooked, insert a knife into the thickest part of the muffin; if it comes out clean, they're done.

Reserve half of the batch for munching now and place the other half in the freezer for up to 3 months. These muffins are perfect to bung in lunchboxes first thing in the morning – they'll be defrosted by midday.

MAKE IT FUN!
Get your little ones to help put all the ingredients into the blender, pressing the on button is always the fun part. If you don't mind a few spillages, they will enjoy spooning the mixture into the muffin cases, too.

SALMON FISHCAKES

Crispy and golden on the outside, soft and flavourful on the inside. Quickly whip together these delicious salmon cakes in no time, a great way to add vitamin- and nutrient-rich fish into our diets.

5 fishcakes

10 minutes

125g (4oz) white potatoes, peeled and cut into 2.5cm (1in) cubes

100g (3½oz) sweet potatoes, peeled and cut into 2.5cm (1in) cubes

200–250g (7–9oz) cooked salmon (use canned or freshly cooked, but ensure to remove any bones and skin)

1 tbsp chopped chives

1 small garlic clove, crushed or grated

1 egg

45g (1½oz) plain (all-purpose) flour

finely grated zest of 1 small lime

70g (2½oz) breadcrumbs

1 tsp sunflower or olive oil

Put the white and sweet potatoes in a microwaveable bowl, add a splash of water and tightly cover the bowl. Steam in the microwave for 5 minutes until tender. You can also boil the potatoes on the hob in a saucepan. Drain and mash until smooth.

Add the salmon, chives, garlic, egg, flour and lime zest, and give it all a good stir, ensuring that you don't break up the salmon too much.

Add the breadcrumbs to a separate bowl.

Take heaped tablespoons of the salmon mixture, roll into a ball with your hands, then place in the breadcrumbs and flatten into a patty shape. Repeat with the rest of the mixture.

Heat the oil in a non-stick frying pan and fry the patties over a medium-high heat for a couple of minutes on each side until the fish cakes have gained a lovely golden crust. All the filling is cooked inside, so you just need to heat it up until piping hot.

Enjoy with a fresh salad or sweet potato and parsnip wedges (see page 81).

These fishcakes will keep for 1 day in the fridge, but ideally can be frozen for up to 2 months. Defrost thoroughly, before reheating in the oven at 180°C fan (200°C/400°F/Gas 6). Bake for 10-15 minutes or until piping hot inside.

COURGETTE PUFF PINWHEELS

Puff pastry pinwheels are a yummy way to pack in lots of veggies in a utterly moreish and irresistible way. I bet you can't just eat one!

EF*

V

🍴 **12 pinwheels**
⏱ **20 minutes**

375g pack of ready-rolled puff pastry
2½ tbsp tomato purée (paste)
1 tsp mixed dried herbs
1 tsp garlic granules
2 tsp smoked paprika
1 small courgette (zucchini)
80g (3oz) Cheddar, grated
1 egg, beaten (optional)*
freshly ground black pepper
baking tray, lined with non-stick baking paper

Preheat the oven to 200°C fan (220°C/425°F/Gas 7).

Take the pastry out of the fridge to come up to room temperature while you prepare the filling.

In a small bowl, add the tomato purée, 5 tbsp water, the herbs, garlic granules, paprika and some black pepper. Stir until well combined and set aside.

Coarsely grate the courgette, then pile into the centre of a clean tea towel. Gather the sides together and squeeze out as much liquid from the courgette as you can. Do this over the sink, as courgettes hold a surprising amount of water. Ensure you don't skip this step as the finished pinwheels will be rather soggy without removing the liquid from the courgette.

Unroll the pastry, then spread the tomato sauce evenly across the entire sheet.

Sprinkle over the squeezed courgette, separating it with your fingers so there aren't any large clumps. Ensure you reach all the edges, so every pinwheel has an equal amount of filling. Sprinkle over the cheese edge-to-edge.

Then, from one of the long sides, roll the pastry into a long sausage, as tight as you can. Using a very sharp knife, cut the roll into 12 equal slices, and place on a lined baking tray, flat-side down, so you can see the spiral design.

Lightly brush each pinwheel with beaten egg, if using (this is optional if you are following an egg-free diet).

Bake in the preheated oven for 15–17 minutes until the pastry has puffed up and turned golden.

These pastries will keep in the fridge for 2 days, or freezer for 3 months. To reheat from frozen, pop a pinwheel on a non-stick baking tray and bake in a hot oven for 5–10 minutes until piping hot all the way through.

BROCCOLI CHEESE BITES

Light and airy cheesy bites with the flavours of a cheese scone but with a nutritious broccoli bonus! Pictured with the courgette puff pinwheels, page 144.

EF*

V

Vg*

DF*

🍴 **24 mini or 12 regular muffins**
⏱ **20-25 minutes**

130g (4½oz) broccoli (around ½ head)
150g (5oz) self-raising (self-rising) flour
1 tsp baking powder
2 eggs or 2 tbsp ground flaxseeds (linseeds) mixed with an extra 75ml (2½fl oz) milk of your choice*
½ tsp smoked paprika
½ tsp mustard powder
70g (2½oz) grated Cheddar or 2 tbsp nutritional yeast, plus extra for topping (optional)*
150ml (5fl oz) milk of your choice*
non-stick 24-hole mini muffin tin, or 12-hole muffin tin, greased

Preheat the oven to 180°C fan (200°C/400°F/Gas 6).

Coarsely grate the broccoli using a box grater or finely chop using a knife. Add to a bowl, cover and microwave for 2 minutes. Alternatively steam the florets on the hob for 5 minutes then cut into small pieces using a knife.

Meanwhile add all the other ingredients to a bowl. Add the broccoli once cooked and drained of any excess moisture. Give it all good mix.

Spoon into the greased muffin tin, sprinkle a little extra cheese on top of each muffin and bake in the preheated oven for 12–15 minutes for minis, or 15–20 minutes for regular-sized muffins. The bites should be golden on top, have risen nicely and spring back when you gently push your finger on the surface. Enjoy!

These bites will keep for 3 days in an airtight container or can be frozen for up to 3 months. Pop one in the microwave to reheat for 60-90 seconds, turning halfway through.

SALT-FREE BABY-FRIENDLY SKINLESS SAUSAGES

DF

These succulent little pork bites are flavoured mildly with smoked paprika and garlic. They are delicious, salt-free, quick and easy to make! Pictured with the baby-friendly meatballs, page 148.

🍴 **2 adults and 3 littles**

⏱ **15 minutes**

500g (1lb 2 oz) 10–20% fat minced (ground) pork
2 tsp smoked paprika
1 tsp garlic granules
1 tsp mixed dried herbs
1 egg
3 heaped tbsp dried breadcrumbs
1 tbsp Worcestershire sauce
freshly ground black pepper
sunflower, vegetable or olive oil, for baking
large baking tray, lined with non-stick baking paper

Preheat the oven to 200°C fan (220°C/425°F/Gas 7).

Put all the ingredients (except the oil) into a large bowl with a good grinding of black pepper, then get your hands into the mixture to squish it all together so the spices and breadcrumbs combine really well with the meat.

Take a golf ball-sized amount of the mixture, and roll it into a smooth ball by cupping both hands and rolling the meat between your palms. Then straighten your hand and roll the meat into a long sausage around 10cm (4in) in length. Repeat with the remaining mixture.

Place each sausage on the lined baking tray, ensuring they aren't touching. Drizzle with a little oil, then bake for 10–15 minutes until golden on the outside and cooked all the way through, turning them halfway through, so the meat colours and cooks evenly. To check that the sausages are cooked, cut one open to check that there is no soft pink meat inside and the juices are running clear.

Cut each sausage in quarters lengthways to serve to babies from 6 months, and in half lengthways from 10 months.

Left over cooked sausages can be kept in the freezer for up to 3 months. Bake from frozen at 180°C fan (200°C/400°F/Gas 6) for 20 minutes, until piping hot inside.

PAN FRYING!
Alternatively, you can pan fry these sausages for 8–10 minutes, turning often, until golden and cooked through.

BABY-FRIENDLY MEATBALLS

Shaping traditional meatballs into long sausage shapes makes them much easier for baby to hold. They will cook in the same time as regular round meatballs, so if you are particular about wanting your meatballs round, feel free to roll half into balls and half into sausages, so the whole family can enjoy this meal together.

🍴 2 adults and 3 littles

⏱ 25 minutes

250g (9oz) 15% fat minced (ground) pork

250g (9oz) 5% fat minced (ground) beef

1 small onion, finely diced

1 heaped tsp garlic granules

40g (1½oz) dried breadcrumbs

1 egg

40g (1½oz) Cheddar, grated

freshly ground black pepper

sunflower, vegetable or olive oil, for baking

large baking tray, lined with non-stick baking paper

Preheat the oven to 220°C fan (240°C/475°F/Gas 9).

Put all the ingredients (except the oil) into a large bowl with a good grinding of black pepper, then get your hands into the mixture to squish it all together, so the onion and breadcrumbs combine really well with the meat. You don't want to be able to see large areas of either pork or beef, so ensure you squish these together, too.

Take a golf ball-sized amount of the mixture, and roll it into a smooth ball by cupping both hands and rolling the meat between your palms. To make a sausage shape, straighten your hand and roll the meat into a long sausage around 7.5cm (3in) in length. Repeat with the remaining mixture.

Place each meatball on the lined baking tray, ensuring they aren't touching. Drizzle with a little oil, then bake for 15–20 minutes until golden on the outside and cooked all the way through, turning them halfway through cooking, so the meat colours and cooks evenly.

Cut each sausage into quarters lengthways to serve to babies from 6 months, and in half lengthways from 10 months. Serve with mashed potatoes, veg and gravy, or in a hidden veg or tomato sauce with pasta (see page 65). They are also great thinly sliced and topped on pizza (see page 51).

Allow to cool fully before placing in a freezer bag and freezing for up to 3 months. Reheat from frozen in the oven at 180°C fan (200°C/400°F/Gas 6) for 10–15 minutes, until piping hot inside.

EASY PRAWN CAKES

Asian-inspired, soft and totally moreish, these little patties are flavoured with succulent prawns, garlic, spring onions, coriander and lime. I really urge you to give these a go –it's a great way to introduce prawns!

🍴 **6 cakes**
⏱ **10 minutes**

165g (5¾oz) fresh raw
   prawns (shrimp)
4 tbsp self-raising
   (self-rising) flour
1 tbsp cornflour
   (cornstarch)
1 large garlic clove,
   roughly chopped
2 spring onions
   (scallions), roughly
   chopped
1 egg or 1 chia egg,
   see page 140*
juice of 1 lime
small handful of
   coriander (cilantro),
   leaves and stalks
1 tbsp olive or sunflower
   oil
freshly ground black
   pepper

Add all the ingredients (apart from the oil) to a food processor with a good grinding of black pepper, then whizz up until you can't see any large pieces of prawns or spring onions.

Heat a large, heavy-bottomed, non-stick frying pan over a medium heat. Once you can feel the heat when hovering your hand over the pan, it's time to cook the prawn cakes.

Scoop tablespoonfuls of the mixture into the pan, using a second spoon to help scrape it into the frying pan. Gently spread into a general circle shape, then add the second cake until you have no room left in the pan (you will probably need to cook these in 2 batches). Ensure you spoon the cakes into the pan fairly quickly, so they all cook at the same time.

Cook for a couple of minutes, then flip each cake over using a sturdy plastic spatula. Once flipped, slightly press on the cake using the back of the spatula to help the cakes cook quickly and evenly. Cook on the second side for another couple of minutes – if they are browning too quickly, reduce the heat.

Once both sides have turned golden and crispy, and the cakes feel firm to the touch, remove from the pan and set aside.

Cut into strips and serve with salad and full-fat Greek-style yogurt for dipping. Adults, try dipping these in sweet chilli sauce!

These prawn cakes will last for 1 day in the fridge, or for up to 2 months in the freezer. Defrost thoroughly before reheating in a hot oven for 10 minutes, or until piping hot inside.

A NOTE ABOUT FREEZING
If you intend to freeze these prawn cakes, ensure the prawns you purchase are suitable for freezing. Any fish or shellfish which has previously been frozen and thawed is not suitable for freezing again.

TUNA AND CHICKPEA HAND-PIES

Here, a mildly spiced, soft tuna and chickpea filling is encased in gloriously flaky pastry. The ultimate finger food the whole family will want seconds of. Best enjoyed warm out of the oven, but equally delicious cold, and great to pack up in lunch boxes!

🍴 6 pies
⏲ 20 minutes

375g pack of ready-rolled puff pastry
400g can chickpeas, drained (liquid reserved*), rinsed and any excess water shaken off
145g can tuna in spring water, drained
1 tsp garlic granules
1 tsp ground coriander
¼ tsp ground cumin
1 tbsp plain (all-purpose) flour
1 beaten egg or the reserved chickpea water*
2 tsp nigella seeds or sesame seeds
freshly ground black pepper

Preheat the oven to 220°C fan (240°C/475°F/Gas 9) and take the pastry out of the fridge to come up to room temperature.

In a large bowl, use a potato masher to mash the chickpeas to a fairly smooth paste. You will still see the skins and a few lumps are totally fine, too – it's nice to have a bit of texture. Add the drained tuna, along with the garlic, coriander, cumin, flour, a good grinding of black pepper and half of the beaten egg (or 1½ tbsp of the chickpea water). Stir until well combined.

Cut the pastry into 6 squares and place on a large non-stick baking tray. Divide the chickpea and tuna mixture into 6 portions and spoon into the centre of each square. Pile the filling high, leaving at least a 1.5cm (½in) gap of pastry around the edge.

Brush a little egg (or chickpea water) around the edge of each pastry square, then fold over diagonally to create little triangles. Crimp the edges with a fork, then brush the tops with more egg or chickpea water. Sprinkle over a few nigella or sesame seeds. Bake for 15–20 minutes until puffed up and golden on top.

Keep in the fridge for 2 days, or freeze for up to 3 months. Defrost well, then pop in a hot oven for 5–10 minutes until piping hot.

CORNFLAKE CHICKEN DIPPERS

Succulent chicken strips with a delicious crispy, smokey and sweet coating, served with a super-quick garlic and lemon "dip-dip". Make a big batch, freeze and pull out on days where time has run away from you.

🍴 **2 adults and 2 littles**

⏱ **25 minutes**

160g (5½oz) cornflakes (about 4 large handfuls)
1 tsp smoked paprika
2 tbsp plain (all-purpose) flour
1 large (US extra-large) beaten egg or 3 tbsp full-fat (whole) milk*
600g (1lb 5oz) chicken, cut into strips (use either breast or skinless, boneless thigh meat)
freshly ground black pepper
sunflower oil, for baking
large baking tray, lined with non-stick baking paper

GARLIC AND LEMON "DIP-DIP"

3 tbsp full-fat Greek-style yogurt or plant-based alternative*
1 garlic clove, grated or crushed
juice of ½ lemon
freshly ground black pepper

Preheat the oven to 180°C fan (200°C/400°F/Gas 6).

Add the cornflakes and smoked paprika to a large sealable food bag, seal, removing most of the air from the bag, and roll over using a rolling pin until all the cornflakes have crushed to a powder. This will only take 30 seconds or so. Transfer the crumb to a medium bowl ready for coating the chicken.

Add the flour, egg and a grinding of black pepper to the chicken and mix using one hand. Then place one piece of chicken into the cornflakes using your wet hand, and coat using your dry hand. Place onto the lined baking tray and repeat.

Ensure each piece of chicken isn't touching any other, then drizzle with a little oil and bake for 15–20 minutes until the chicken is cooked through and the crust has gained a lovely golden colour.

Meanwhile make the dip, by mixing all the ingredients together in a small bowl.

Serve the dippers and their dip with smoked paprika sweet potato and parsnip wedges (see page 81).

The dip will keep in the fridge for 3–4 days; just stir before serving. The dippers last up to 3 months in the freezer. When needed, pop a couple of chicken dippers in a hot oven to cook from frozen for 15–20 minutes, or until piping hot all the way through.

LENTIL SPAG BOL

Packed full of flavour, this simple vegetarian midweek meal is ready in just 30 minutes!

EF

V*

Vg*

DF

🍴 2 adults and 2 littles

⏱ 30 minutes

1 tbsp olive or sunflower oil

1 large onion, finely diced

3 carrots, finely diced

3 garlic cloves, crushed

1 tbsp tomato purée (paste)

500g (1lb 2oz) passata (strained tomatoes)

350g pack of green lentils in water (no added salt)

2 tsp dried mixed herbs

1 tsp smoked paprika

1 low-salt vegetable or chicken stock cube*

freshly ground black pepper

Heat the oil in a large saucepan, add the onion and cook over a medium heat for 2 minutes, stirring often so the onion doesn't catch.

Add the carrots and cook together for a further 4 minutes, stirring often.

Add the garlic and tomato purée, and cook for another minute, then add the passata, lentils (including the packet water), the mixed herbs, smoked paprika and a good grinding of black pepper, and crumble in the stock cube.

Give it all a good stir, pop a lid on and simmer for 20 minutes until the carrots have softened and the flavours have mingled.

Serve with freshly cooked pasta, a sprinkling of grated cheese on top and steamed veg on the side.

To serve to baby, spoon a small amount into a separate flat-bottomed cold pan, roughly mash with a potato masher, then add a little pasta and cover in the sauce. Choose a long, easy pasta shape for baby to hold, like rigatoni or spirals. You can also blend up the sauce with a little of the pasta to make a purée for baby.

Freeze any leftover lentil spag bol in portions for up to 4 months. Defrost thoroughly and reheat in a saucepan with an extra splash of water, until bubbling and piping hot.

Snacks and Puds

TEETHING BISCUITS

Slightly soft in texture, these biscuits crumble easily, and are mild in flavour. Perfect for babies from 6 months of age to help ease their sore gums. Got all your teeth now? These biscuits are delicious dunked into yogurt or peanut butter for a healthy mummy or daddy snack!

GF

EF

V

Vg

DF

🍴 **10 biscuits**

⏱ **30 minutes**

180g (6oz) rolled (old-fashioned) porridge oats
1 banana
2 tbsp coconut oil
½ tsp ground cinnamon (optional)
1 tsp pure vanilla extract (optional)

Preheat the oven to 170°C fan (190°C/375°F/Gas 5).

Place the oats in a food processor and blend to the consistency of fine breadcrumbs. Add the rest of the ingredients and whizz until combined.

Tip out onto a clean work surface and bring the dough together with your hands; it should come together easily, but if it doesn't, return to the food processor, add a touch more coconut oil or banana and whizz together.

Flatten out to about 1.5cm (⅔in) thick with the palm of your hands, and cut into 10 strips. Take each piece of mixture and form into a long biscuit (cookie) with rounded corners. Get older siblings to help shape the biscuits for their baby brother or sister. Your little chef will love modelling the biscuits, it's a little like playing with modelling dough.

Place onto a non-stick baking tray and bake in the preheated oven for 20–30 minutes, flipping halfway through. Allow to cool completely before serving to baby.

Store the biscuits in an airtight container for up to 1 week.

GINGER OAT COOKIES

Soft little bakes, mildly spiced with ginger. These are the perfect breakfast or snack to pack up and feed baby on the go.

🍴 **15 cookies**

⏱ **15 minutes**

200g (7oz) rolled (old-fashioned) porridge oats

100g (3½oz) plain (all-purpose) flour

1 tsp bicarbonate of soda (baking soda)

3 tsp ground ginger

75ml (2½fl oz) honey or maple syrup* (optional, honey should only be served to babies over 12 months)

100g (3½oz) unsalted butter or coconut oil, melted*

1 tsp pure vanilla extract

90g (3oz) 100% apple purée (homemade or a baby pouch)

baking tray, lined with non-stick baking paper

Preheat the oven to 200°C fan (220°C/425°F/Gas 7).

To a large mixing bowl, add the oats, flour, bicarbonate of soda and ground ginger. Roughly mix until all combined.

Add the honey, melted butter, vanilla extract and apple purée to the oats and give it all a good stir.

Take small amounts of the mixture in your hands and roll into golf ball-sized shapes. Place onto the lined baking tray and gently press the balls down with your hand to flatten each cookie to around 1.5cm (½in) in thickness.

Bake for 8–12 minutes until golden. The cookies will feel very soft coming out of the oven, but will harden slightly as they cool.

Store the cookies in an airtight container for up to 5 days or freeze for up to 3 months.

PEANUT BUTTER SOFT-BAKE COOKIES

These soft little cookies are packed full of addictive peanut butter and comforting banana flavours. Pictured with ginger oat cookies, page 163.

🍴 12 cookies
⏱ 15 minutes

1 banana, about 80g (3oz)
150g (5½oz) smooth
   100% peanut butter
1 egg
1 tsp pure vanilla extract
1 tbsp honey or maple
   syrup (optional, honey
   should only be served
   to babies over 12
   months)
170g (6oz) rolled
   (old-fashioned)
   porridge oats
baking tray, lined with
   non-stick baking paper

Preheat the oven to 180°C fan (200°C/400°F/Gas 6).

Mash the banana in a large bowl, then add the peanut butter, egg, vanilla and honey. Stir, then pour in the oats and mix until well combined.

Roll into golf ball-sized rounds and place on a lined baking tray, at least 5cm (2in) apart. The mixture will be sticky, so it may help to clean your hands halfway through rolling the mixture.

Using the back of a fork, gently press each ball down to flatten slightly, then pop the cookies in the oven for 12–14 minutes until slightly golden on the outside, still soft on the inside but fully cooked throughout.

Store the cookies in an airtight container for up to 5 days or freeze for up to 3 months.

CINNAMON AND BANANA OATY CUPS

These soft and delicious oat bites are a great alternative to porridge.

🍴 24 minis or
   12 regular cups
⏱ 20-25 minutes

1 banana
2 tbsp ground flaxseeds
   (linseeds)
1 tsp ground cinnamon
6 tbsp rolled (old-
   fashioned) porridge
   oats
10 tbsp milk*
24-hole mini muffin pan,
   greased

Preheat the oven to 180°C fan (200°C/400°F/Gas 6).

Mash the banana in a large bowl, then mix in the rest of the ingredients (use plant-based milk if vegan).

Spoon into the muffin mould or greased tin. Bake for 20 minutes for minis or 25 minutes for regular-sized muffins.

Serve with fresh fruit, and full-fat Greek-style yogurt (or plant-based alternative*) for dipping.

Store the cups in an airtight container for up to 4 days or freeze for up to 3 months.

CARROT AND APPLE SOFT OATY BARS

Soft little sugar-free bars packed full of fruit and veg. Whip up a batch at the start of the week and you have an easy grab breakfast or snack for the next few days!

🍴 18 bars
⏱ 20 minutes

1 large apple
1 large carrot
270g (9½oz) rolled
  (old-fashioned)
  porridge oats
50g (1¾oz) soft coconut
  oil or unsalted butter*
45g (1¾oz) 100% apple
  purée (homemade or a
  baby pouch)
100g (3½oz) (dark) raisins
2 heaped tsp ground
  cinnamon
2 tsp pure vanilla extract
1 tsp baking powder
20cm (8in) brownie tin,
  greased and lined with
  a strip of non-stick
  baking paper that
  overhangs on opposite
  ends

Preheat the oven to 180°C fan (200°C/400°F/Gas 6).

Grate the apple on a box grater (no need to remove the skin, but be sure to grate around the centre core and discard this). Then remove the ends of the carrot and grate this too (no need to peel as long as you have washed it well).

Add the grated apple and carrot to a blender (including any juice which has released onto your board), then add the rest of the ingredients. Whizz up until most of the raisins have been chopped in half.

Spoon into your lined tin, then, using the back of a metal dinner spoon, spread the mixture to all sides of the tin and flatten the top so it's an even layer all over.

Bake on the middle shelf of the oven for 15–20 minutes until just starting to turn darker around the edges.

Remove from the oven, then lift the whole bake out of the tray using the baking paper, and place on a wire rack for 5 minutes to lower the temperature.

Then slide the bake onto a flat surface, before cutting into 18 finger-sized slices. These bars will last for up to a week stored in an airtight container.

DIP TIP!
Try these bars dipped in full-fat Greek-style or plant-based yogurt!

PEANUT BUTTER AND BANANA FLAPJACKS

So deliciously soft and moreish! Swap the usual sugary golden syrup with bananas and peanut butter for a gorgeous flavour combo that the whole family will love.

🍴 15 flapjacks
⏱ 20 minutes

80g (3oz) coconut oil
2 ripe bananas
3 tbsp 100% peanut
    butter, smooth or
    crunchy
40g (1½oz) honey or
    maple syrup*
    (optional, honey
    should only be served
    to babies over 12
    months)
300g (10½oz) rolled
    (old-fashioned)
    porridge oats
40g (1½oz) desiccated
    (dried unsweetened
    shredded) coconut
70g (2½oz) (dark) raisins
50g (1¾oz) dark
    (bittersweet)
    chocolate, to decorate
    (optional)*
20cm (8in) brownie tin,
    greased and lined with
    a strip of non-stick
    baking paper that
    overhangs on opposite
    ends

Preheat the oven to 180°C fan (200°C/400°F/Gas 6).

Measure the coconut oil into a small bowl and microwave for a minute until melted.

Meanwhile, add the bananas to a large mixing bowl and mash with the back of a fork. Now stir in the peanut butter, melted coconut oil and honey or maple syrup until well combined.

Add the oats, desiccated coconut and raisins, and stir well until all the wet ingredients have mixed into the dry.

Tip the mixture into a lined square brownie tin. Using the back of a metal tablespoon, compact the mixture down while evenly distributing the oats, so you have a level flapjack.

Bake in the preheated oven for 15–20 minutes until the edges have started to turn golden. The middle will feel very soft, however as the bake cools the mixture will stay together.

Let it sit for a couple of minutes, then remove the flapjack from the tin using the baking paper to lift the entire bake and place onto a large chopping board. Cut into 15 rectangles and transfer to a wire rack.

As an optional extra, once the flapjack has cooled, melt the dark chocolate and sporadically drizzle over the flapjack pieces using a spoon.

Store in an airtight container for up to 5 days.

BLUEBERRY SPONGE FINGERS

Soft, delicious sponge, bejewelled with juicy, flavourful blueberries, this is so low in sugar, I even serve it up for breakfast to my Nina.

🍴 **12 fingers**

⏱ **25 minutes**

90g (3oz) shop-bought 100% apple purée (use a baby food pouch) or 1 medium mashed banana

60g (2oz) rolled (old-fashioned) porridge oats

225g (8oz) self-raising (self-rising) flour

1 tsp baking powder

2 tsp pure vanilla extract

40g (1½oz) fruit sugar or golden caster (superfine) sugar

200g (7oz) baking spread or softened unsalted butter

3 eggs

130g (4½oz) blueberries

20cm (8in) brownie tin, greased and lined with a strip of non-stick baking paper that overhangs on opposite ends

Preheat the oven to 180°C fan (200°C/400°F/Gas 6).

Add all the ingredients, except the blueberries, to a large bowl and mix using an electric whisk until just combined. Be sure not to over-mix, as this works the gluten in the flour too much, resulting in a dense cake.

Pour the batter into the lined tin, and spread out using the back of a spoon so the mixture reaches the corners.

Scatter over the blueberries evenly, and gently push the berries into the batter a little.

Bake on the middle shelf of the oven for 20–22 minutes, or until an inserted knife comes out clean.

Lift the cake out the tin using the baking paper and transfer onto a wire rack to cool, before cutting in half down the middle, then into 12 long fingers.

Store in an airtight container for up to 3 days.

EGG-FREE BANANA CUSTARD

Dip those blueberry sponge fingers from page 169 into this baby-friendly, sugar-free, banana custard.

🍴 **2 adults and 2 littles**
⏱ **10 minutes**

2 bananas
600ml (1 pint) milk
    of your choice*, plus
    2 tbsp
2 tsp pure vanilla extract
2 heaped tbsp cornflour
    (cornstarch)

Add the bananas to a saucepan. Using a potato masher, mash the bananas until you have a fairly smooth paste. Add the milk and vanilla extract, then put onto to a medium-high heat, whisking well to ensure the banana is mixed into the milk.

The banana will add a slight texture to the custard, so if you prefer a completely smooth consistency, use a hand-held blender to give the banana milk a whizz up while it's coming up to heat.

While you wait for the milk to warm up, take a small bowl, and add the cornflour. Add the extra 2 tbsp milk into the cornflour and stir until you have a runny paste.

Once the milk is starting to simmer, quickly pour the cornflour mixture into the warm milk, then use a whisk to stir the custard quickly and constantly until it thickens. This should take 3–5 minutes.

If the custard is too thick, add a splash of milk to loosen the consistency. Equally, if your custard hasn't thickened much, mix up an extra tablespoon of the cornflour slurry and add this to the custard. Do note however, the custard will thicken as it cools.

Keep in the fridge for 3 days, or freeze in portions for up to 3 months. Defrost and warm up with a tiny splash of extra milk to help loosen the consistency.

FRUIT SALAD WITH LIME YOGURT "DIP-DIP"

Fruit salad is a great way to dress up healthy fruit in a way that makes it more appealing to fussy eaters. Pick a variety of fruit that is in season and serve alongside this tastebud-tingling yogurt dip.

GF

EF

V

Vg*

DF*

🍴 **2 adults and 2 littles**
⏱ **10 minutes**

FRUIT SALAD

about 5 handfuls of chopped fruit, such as mango, kiwi, blueberries, strawberries, banana, pineapple, raspberries, satsuma segments, grapes, pear, nectarine, watermelon, honeydew melon, Galia melon or cherries
juice of 1 orange

YOGURT "DIP-DIP"

400g (14oz) full-fat Greek yogurt or coconut yogurt*
finely grated zest and juice of ½ lime
2 tbsp honey or maple syrup* (optional, honey should only be served to babies over 12 months)

Cut all fruit into finger strips if you're serving to newly weaning babies. Remove skins and any centres that are tough or seedy. Once your child is a confident eater, larger chunks will be fine.

Mango: Hold the fruit on its side, find the middle point and move to the left or right by 1cm (½in), then cut down, trying to move around the centre stone (pit). You will now have a large piece of mango, skin still on. Repeat for the other-side. The centre piece is the cook's treat! Slice each mango half into wedges lengthways, then run your knife under each wedge to remove the skin.

Kiwi: Top and tail using a paring knife, then cut away the skin. Cut the kiwi in half lengthways, then into wedges.

Pineapple: Top and tail the pineapple. Stand it flat on a chopping board and gently run your knife down the side of the pineapple about 5mm (¼in) in to remove the skin. If you have lots of eyes left, remove them using the end of a sharp knife. Slice big chunks of the pineapple, ensuring to cut around the centre tough core. Then slice each large chunk into strips. You can also buy canned pineapple rings in fruit juice – just cut each ring in half.

Grapes, cherries and strawberries: Quarter lengthways, removing stones (pits) from cherries.

Raspberries: Serve whole or tear in half as they are super soft.

Blueberries: These should be halved or squished.

Bananas: These can be cut in half, then separated into 3 sections by pushing your finger down the centre seam of the fruit.

Satsumas: Either cut into small pieces, or peel each segment. You can also purchase tinned satsuma segments in fruit juice.

Melon: Melons should be cut into strips and the skin removed.

Add all the chopped fruit to a large bowl, along with the juice of 1 orange. Gently toss and set aside for 10 minutes to marinate. Mix the yogurt "dip-dip" ingredients together and serve.

CARROT AND RAISIN MUFFINS

A great way to get in some extra veggies, even at breakfast. Make a big batch and you have a quick-grab snack for the rest of the week.

EF*

V

Vg*

DF*

🍴 **12 muffins**

⏱ **25 minutes**

260g (9oz) carrots, coarsely grated (about 4 medium carrots)

200g (7oz) self-raising (self-rising) flour

1 tsp baking powder

2 tsp pure vanilla extract

2 tsp ground cinnamon

80g (3oz) unsalted butter or coconut oil*, softened

50g (1¾oz) maple syrup (optional)

3 eggs or 3 chia eggs, see page 140*

80g (3oz) (dark) raisins, tossed in 1 tbsp plain (all-purpose) flour

12-hole muffin tin, lined with paper cases

Preheat the oven to 180°C fan (200°C/400°F/Gas 6).

Place the grated carrots in a bowl and add all the other ingredients (except the raisins). Give it a good stir, but try not to over-mix. Add the raisins tossed in flour and briefly stir into the cake batter – this helps prevent the raisins from sinking to the bottom of the muffins.

Spoon the mixture into the lined muffin tin and bake for 20–25 minutes until well risen, and an inserted skewer comes out clean.

Store in an airtight container for up to 5 days or freeze for up to 3 months.

ALMOND AND PRUNE MUFFINS

Deliciously soft almond muffins jam packed with juicy prune pieces. These little pillows of Bakewell inspired deliciousness pack up really well for snacks when out and about!

🍴 **12 muffins or 24 mini muffins**

⏱ **20 minutes**

290g can pitted prunes in apple juice, or 175g (6oz) drained canned prunes and 115ml (4fl oz) apple juice or purée

80g (3oz) ground almonds

2 heaped tbsp milled flaxseeds (linseeds)

120g (4oz) self-raising (self-rising) flour

1 tbsp maple or fruit syrup

1 tsp baking powder

3 tsp almond extract

1 tsp pure vanilla extract

3 eggs or 3 chia eggs, see page 140*

2 tbsp, plus 1 tsp milk of your choice*

70g (2½oz) unsalted butter or coconut oil*, melted

12-hole muffin tin, lined with paper cases, or 24-hole mini muffin mould, greased

Preheat the oven to 180°C fan (200°C/400°F/Gas 6).

Add the prunes to a large bowl, and slightly break up a little using the back of a spoon. Add the rest of the ingredients and stir until just combined, but try not to over-mix.

Divide the mixture between the muffin cases or mini muffin mould. Bake for 15–20 minutes for large muffins 14–16 minutes for mini muffins.

Store in an airtight container for up to 5 days or freeze for up to 3 months.

NUTRITION NOTE

When babies start to move onto solid foods from exclusively feeding on milk, it isn't uncommon for them to experience harder stools for a couple of weeks while their digestive system adjusts to more solid textured foods. Fruits such as prunes can help with constipation, as they have a natural laxative effect to help keep everything regular. If you are concerned, seek professional advice.

BABY BLISS BALLS FOUR WAYS

Bliss balls are a versatile healthy treat usually consisting of nuts and dried fruit. Try these four combinations with the addition of oats or almond flour, making the gorgeous bites super-soft. You can either roll them in a traditional ball shape, or into a sausage if serving to little ones, which may be easier for them to hold.

🍴 **10 small balls each**
⏱ **5 minutes**

PEANUT BUTTER AND CHOCOLATE

110g (4oz) rolled
   (old-fashioned)
   porridge oats
2 tbsp coconut oil
2 heaped tbsp 100%
   peanut butter
2 tbsp unsweetened
   cocoa powder
14 dried dates or prunes
4 heaped tbsp desiccated
   (dried unsweetened
   shredded) coconut

CARROT CAKE

1 carrot, finely grated and
   the juice squeezed out
   (about 50g (1¾oz)
   drained weight)
80g (3oz) rolled
   (old-fashioned)
   porridge oats
55g (2oz) (dark) raisins
30g (1oz) coconut oil
1 tsp ground cinnamon
pinch of ground nutmeg
65g (2¼oz) ground
   almonds
4 heaped tbsp desiccated
   (dried unsweetened
   shredded) coconut

MANGO AND CASHEW

100g (3½oz)
   unsweetened soft
   dried mango
60g (2oz) cashew nuts
juice of 1 lemon
1 tbsp chia seeds
3 tbsp rolled (old-
   fashioned) porridge
   oats
4 heaped tbsp desiccated
   (dried unsweetened
   shredded) coconut

APRICOT, WALNUT AND GINGER

200g (7oz) unsweetened
   dried apricots
30g (1oz) coconut oil
50g (1¾oz) walnut pieces
30g (1oz) coconut flour or
   ground almonds
1 tsp ground ginger

Add all the ingredients (except the coconut) to a food processor and whizz up until the mixture starts to clump together. The mango and cashew mixture may take around 5 minutes of blending for the ingredients to bind together, depending on how powerful your machine is.

If using coconut, add it to a small bowl ready for rolling.

Take a walnut-sized amount of the mixture and roll into a smooth ball in your hand. Flatten the ball and roll it into a sausage shape. Add the bliss ball to the coconut and roll until it's all covered. Repeat with the remaining mixture.

All bliss balls will keep in an airtight container and store in a cool dry place for up to 5–7 days.

NUTRITION NOTE

Apricots are really high in fibre, and a great addition to a balanced diet.

CHIA CHEESE CRACKERS

Deliciously moreish, these melt-in-the-mouth cheese crackers are quick to whip together, and will keep for up to a week in an air-tight container (although they probably won't stick around that long!).

🍴 **70–100 crackers**
⏱ **15 minutes**

220g (8oz) plain (all-purpose) flour, plus extra for dusting
½ tsp cayenne pepper (don't worry, the crackers won't be spicy)
1 heaped tsp smoked paprika
140g (5oz) unsalted butter, cut into cubes and chilled
240g (9oz) Cheddar, grated
3 heaped tbsp chia seeds
1 small (US medium) beaten egg or 1 tbsp ground flaxseeds (linseeds) mixed with 2½ tbsp warm water*

CREAM CHEESE AND CHIVE DIP

130g (4½oz) full-fat cream cheese
90g (3oz) full-fat Greek-style yogurt
1 heaped tbsp finely chopped chives
1 small garlic clove, finally crushed
pinch of ground white pepper

Preheat the oven to 200°C fan (220°C/425°F/Gas 7).

Add the flour, cayenne, smoked paprika and butter to a food processor, and blitz until it resembles fine breadcrumbs, ensuring not to over-mix.

Add the cheese and chia seeds, and blitz again briefly until combined. Now add the egg, a little at a time, until the dough comes together (you may not need all the egg).

Tip the dough out onto a floured work surface, and quickly form into a ball.

Cut into 4, and roll out each section to around 3mm (⅛in) thick, dusting with flour as you go. Keep moving the dough between each roll to ensure you get an even thickness and to stop it from sticking to the surface.

Use a cookie cutter shape the crackers. You can also use a dinner knife to cut the dough into finger-size strips. Gather up and re-roll any excess dough.

Place the crackers on a non-stick baking tray and prod each one with a fork or chopstick (this ensures the crackers don't puff up too much in the oven).

Bake for 8–10 minutes until coloured slightly and crisped up. Check after 8 minutes as these can catch quickly.

To make the dip, mix all the ingredients together and serve alongside the crackers.

The crackers will last in an airtight container for up to 1 week and the dip will keep in the fridge for up to 3 days.

TIME SAVER!
This mixture makes around 70–100 crackers, depending on the size of your cutters. Before rolling out, cut the dough in half and freeze one section for another day.

SEEDED OAT CAKES

A salt-free version of our favourite Scottish oat cakes, with the addition of seeds for added flavour. Top with cream cheese, mashed fruits, peanut butter or full-fat Greek-style yogurt for a quick-grab lunch or snack on those busy days!

🍴 **26 oatcakes**
⏲ **20 minutes**

200g (7oz) rolled
   (old-fashioned)
   porridge oats
1 heaped tbsp plain
   (all-purpose) flour
80g (3oz) unsalted butter
   or use coconut oil*
100g (3½oz) sesame
   seeds
40g (1½oz) poppy seeds
100g (3½oz) flaxseeds
   (linseeds)
60–100ml (2–3½fl oz)
   warm water
baking tray, lined with
   non-stick baking paper

Preheat the oven to 180°C fan (200°C/400°F/Gas 6).

Add the oats, flour and butter to a food processor and whizz up until it resembles fine breadcrumbs.

Add the seeds and 60ml (2fl oz) of the water, and pulse until the mixture comes together. If you can still see dry crumbs, add a splash more water and blitz again until the dough comes together.

Tip the mixture out onto a floured work surface, and bring it together into a ball with your hands.

Flour the top of the dough ball and a rolling pin, then gently roll the mixture out to 3mm (⅛in) thick. Keep moving the dough as you roll, so it doesn't stick to your work surface. You may need to dust with a little extra flour as you go.

Using a sharp knife, trim the dough into a neat rectangle, removing any jagged edges. Now cut the dough into 2.5 x 7.5cm (1 x 3in) strips. Alternatively use a cookie cutter to shape the oat cakes. Gather up any excess dough, re-roll and cut out some more.

Transfer the oat cakes to the lined baking tray, and bake for 15–20 minutes until the oat cakes have gained a slight golden colour.

These oat cakes will last in an airtight container for up to 10 days.

NUTRITION NOTE
Seeds are an excellent source of fibre and healthy fats, essential to a well-balanced diet.

SPICED SODA BREAD ROLLS

Salt-free delicious bread rolls, with hot cross bun vibes. Swap the cinnamon and mixed spice for 60g (2oz) grated cheese for a savoury option.

EF

V

Vg*

DF*

🍴 **6 buns**
⏲ **20 minutes**

290ml (10fl oz)
   buttermilk or
   plant-based yogurt*
350g (12oz) self-raising
   (self-rising) flour, plus
   extra for dusting
2 tsp mixed spice
2 tsp ground cinnamon
½ tsp bicarbonate of soda
   (baking soda)
2 tbsp full-fat (whole)
   milk or plant-based
   alternative
baking tray, lined with
   non-stick baking paper

Preheat the oven to 200°C fan (220°C/425°F/Gas 7).

Mix all the dry ingredients together in a large bowl, then make a well in the centre and pour in the buttermilk. Using a wooden spoon, start to stir the buttermilk, incorporating the flour into the liquid. When it comes together into a dough, tip it out onto a clean work surface. If you find the mixture is too dry and not coming together, add a splash of milk.

Knead the dough very briefly until it comes together in a small ball. Using a sharp knife, cut it into 6 equal sections.

Take each piece of dough and roll into a ball – try to stretch it into a smooth, neat ball by tucking any excess dough underneath, so the top is stretched and round.

Place each dough ball on the lined baking tray and dust with a little flour. Then, using a sharp knife, score a line over the top of each roll – this helps the buns to rise evenly.

Bake for 18–20 minutes until risen and golden on top. To test whether the buns are cooked, carefully turn one upside down and tap the centre with your finger; if it sound hollow, the buns are cooked.

Allow to cool for 10 minutes before serving.

Store in an airtight container for a couple of days. If the buns have become a little stale, sprinkle with a little water and bake in a hot oven for 5–10 minutes until hot again.

MAKE IT CHEESY!
Swap the mixed spice and cinnamon here for 70g (3oz) cheese to create a delicious savoury roll.

CREAMY MANGO AND RASPBERRY ICE LOLLIES

*Fantastic for teething, this recipe for homemade sugar-free ice lollies is such
a versatile, quick and easy recipe. Whizz up a delicious fruit smoothie with
yogurt for extra creaminess and nutritional goodness, then simply spoon
into any ice pop mould you have, freeze and get stuck in.*

🍴 **4 lollies**

⏱ **4 hours**

250g (9oz) chopped
    mango
100g (3½oz) full-fat
    Greek-style yogurt or
    use a plant-based
    alternative*, plus 1
    tbsp
70g (2½oz) raspberries

Add the mango and 100g (3½oz) yogurt to a food processor,
and whizz up until super smooth.

Meanwhile, mash the raspberries with the back of a fork in a
small bowl, then stir through the 1 tbsp yogurt.

You can now fill any ice lolly mould you have. Small, baby lolly
moulds with easy-grip handles are available to buy, or silicone
push-up-style moulds. Traditional wooden lolly stick moulds work
really well for this quantity.

Spoon a couple of tablespoons of the mango mixture into your
mould to fill it three-quarters of the way up. Then add the
raspberry yogurt to fill the mould. Use the back of a teaspoon to
gently ripple the two colours together. Seal the mould and freeze
for a minimum of 4 hours or ideally overnight.

If you have any leftover mixture, this is delicious served as is with
a spoon, and will keep for 24 hours in the fridge.

WANT MORE FLAVOUR IDEAS?
Ice lollies are a delicious way to sneak in some extra greens. Add
a handful of fresh spinach to the food processor, or the flesh of
an avocado works really well, too. Head to page 48-49 and try
freezing the smoothie bowl and flavoured yogurt mixtures.

CHOCOLATE, PEANUT BUTTER AND BANANA ICE CREAM

Smooth, creamy, melt-in-the-mouth ice cream – minus the cream! Packed full of the good stuff, this delicious little treat has zero guilt attached!

🍴 3 adults and 3 littles
⏲ 10 minutes

4 ripe bananas (about 600g (1lb 5oz) peeled weight), chopped and frozen
100g (3½oz) smooth 100% peanut butter
60g (2oz) unsweetened cocoa powder
130ml (4½fl oz) unsweetened soya (soy) or full-fat (whole) milk*

Add all the ingredients to a powerful food processor and blend until smooth. If your food processor is struggling, wait 5–10 minutes to let the bananas defrost a little, then whizz up in stages, using a spatula to mix between each set of pulsing.

Either serve soft straight away, or transfer to a container and freeze for up to 3 months. Remove from the freezer 45 minutes before you intend to eat to allow the ice cream to soften.

Serve in a bowl with a spoon or scooped in an ice cream cone, or spoon into ice lolly moulds to make deliciously creamy ice pops!

BERRY BANANA ICE POPS

Banana dipped in a simple but delicious berry yogurt and frozen makes a gorgeous and creamy snack. Great for little teething babas or after school treats in the summer.

GF

EF

V

Vg*

DF*

🍴 4 ice pops

⏱ 5-10 minutes, plus chilling

2 bananas
handful of raspberries, blueberries or blackberries
3 tbsp full-fat Greek-style yogurt or plant-based alternative*
4 wooden ice lolly sticks or 4 children's forks

OPTIONAL TOPPINGS
melted dark chocolate, for drizzling
passion fruit
freeze dried raspberries
flaked (sliced) almonds
baby granola powder, see page 28

Cut each banana in half, and stick a wooden lolly stick halfway into each half (from the cut end).

Lay flat in a box or on a plate, and put in the freezer for at least 1 hour.

Meanwhile, make the yogurt coating by mashing your chosen berries with the back of a fork and mixing in the yogurt. Decant into a slim tall glass or jug (pitcher).

Take the bananas out of the freezer and dip into the yogurt mixture. Pop back into the freezer for at least 3 hours, or until frozen through.

To serve you can top with added extras, however these frozen banana lollies will be absolutely delicious as is.

KEEP IT COOL!
As they melt (which takes around 10 minutes), the banana and smoothie become really soft, but they will still be lovely and cold.

BAKED BANANAS

Warm, sweet, soft and utterly delicious! Think bananas, but upgraded 100 times. The baked flesh mashes easily with a fork – perfect to offer babies from 6 months.

GF
EF
V
Vg
DF

🍴 **1 adult and 2 littles**
⏱ **15 minutes**

2 large ripe bananas (under-
    ripe bananas won't work
    for this recipe)
1 tsp ground cinnamon
¼ tsp ground mixed spice
olive or coconut oil cooking spray
baking tray, lined with
    non-stick baking paper

Preheat the oven to 180°C fan (200°C/400°F/Gas 6).

Slice the bananas in half lengthways with the skin still on. Place each banana half, skin-side down, onto the lined baking tray. Spray each banana a couple of times with cooking spray, then sprinkle over the cinnamon and mixed spice.

Bake in the preheated oven for 10–15 minutes until the skin has blackened and you can see the sugars in the banana starting to bubble.

Serve with a dollop of full-fat Greek-style yogurt and a few pomegranate seeds, if you like. It is also nice served with drizzles of peanut butter, some sprinkled desiccated (dried unsweetened shredded) coconut or crushed nuts, or even with the super simple chocolate and banana ice cream on page 180 for that irresistible hot-and-cold combo.

WINTER-SPICED POACHED PLUMS AND PEARS

A hug in a bowl! The perfect winter pudding, and if you end up with any leftovers, top it on freshly made porridge the next morning... thank me later!

🍴 2 adults and 2 littles
⏱ 20 minutes

300g (10oz) plums (about 5 plums)
300g (10oz) pears (about 4 pears)
1 cinnamon stick, or 1 heaped tsp ground cinnamon
1 vanilla pod, or 2 tsp pure vanilla extract
40g (1½oz) unrefined sugar, such as maple syrup or golden caster (superfine) sugar (optional)

Wash and quarter each plum, discarding the stone (pit) inside. Peel the pears, cut into quarters lengthways, remove the stem and scoop out the middle core. Add to a medium saucepan along with the plums, cinnamon, vanilla, syrup and 220ml (7½fl oz) water.

Place on a medium heat and simmer with the lid on for 20 minutes, stirring once or twice.

Top with full-fat Greek-style yogurt and lots of the warm juice from the pan.

You can mash for baby or serve as is, as the fruit is really soft.

TRANSFORM IT!
This is fantastic mashed and served on toast, or double up the quantity and top with a crumble oat topping for a delicious family pudding. You could also whip up some toasted oat crumb from page 34 to serve alongside the poached fruit.

MINI RASPBERRY CLAFOUTIS

These sweet little French puddings are like a set egg custard. Traditionally they are made in a big pan, but these mini versions cook in much less time and are easier for babies to hold and eat themselves.

🍽 12 clafoutis
⏱ 25 minutes

4 eggs
100g (3½oz) plain (all-purpose) flour
40g (1½oz) unsalted butter, melted
200ml (7fl oz) full-fat (whole) milk or plant-based alternative
1 tsp pure vanilla extract
1 tbsp maple or agave syrup
200g (7oz) raspberries, see below
1 tbsp icing (confectioners') sugar, to serve (optional)
12-hole non-stick muffin tin, greased with olive or coconut oil cooking spray

Preheat the oven to 180°C fan (200°C/400°F/Gas 6).

Add the flour, eggs, melted butter, milk, vanilla and syrup to a food processor and whizz up until smooth. Set aside to rest for 5 minutes.

Distribute the raspberries between the 12 muffin holes. Pour in the batter so that it comes two-thirds of the way up in each muffin hole.

Bake in the preheated oven for 15–20 minutes until puffed up and starting to turn golden on top.

Let the clafoutis sit in the tin for 5 minutes before gently easing away at the sides and removing from the tin. Don't be alarmed when they sink back down as they cool; this is the desired effect.

To serve, dust with an optional sprinkling of icing sugar, and cut into strips so it's easier for baby to hold.

GOT A SWEET TOOTH?
The raspberries give a delicious sharp and zingy tastes to these little egg custards, however, if you prefer a sweeter taste, opt for blueberries instead.

APPLE AND BLACKBERRY MINI GALETTE

The smell of your kitchen while you bake these utterly delicious and comforting little open-topped pies will make you smile! A fantastic end to a family meal, which baby and grandparents will devour! Use cooking apples, which break down to a lovely soft texture, perfect for baby.

🍴 **6 galette**

⏱ **25 minutes**

375g pack of ready-rolled shortcrust pastry (or use homemade, if you have time)
1 large cooking apple
90g (3oz) blackberries, halved lengthways
1 tbsp cornflour (cornstarch)
1 tsp pure vanilla extract
1 tbsp coconut or unrefined brown sugar, plus extra for sprinkling (optional)
1 beaten egg or 4 tsp milk of your choice*
large baking tray, lined with non-stick baking paper

Preheat the oven to 200°C fan (220°C/425°F/Gas 7) and take the pastry out of the fridge to come up to room temperature a little.

Peel the cooking apple, cut into quarters and remove the core. Slice each quarter into 3mm (⅛in) wide pieces, and pop the sliced apple into a small bowl along with half of the blackberries.

Add the cornflour, vanilla and sugar, and give it a good stir so everything is coated well.

Unroll the pastry, and cut it into 6 squares. Put each piece of pastry onto the lined baking tray – don't worry if they seem too close as you will be folding the pastry up and making it smaller.

Divide the fruit mixture between the 6 pieces of pastry, trying to mound the fruit high in the middle and leaving at least 2.5cm (1in) of pastry exposed around the edge.

Fold the pastry up over the fruit as much as possible, ensuring each edge has folded over a little bit, but leaving the fruit in the middle of the tart exposed.

Brush any exposed pastry with the beaten egg. Sprinkle with the tiniest amount of sugar to help give the pastry a little sweetness.

Bake for 20–25 minutes until the pastry is golden and the fruit is soft.

Best served warm, with a drizzle of cream if you're feeling luxurious or my banana chocolate ice cream (see page 180).

Cut into strips to serve to baby.

SEMOLINA PUDDING
WITH A QUICK NO-SUGAR SUMMER FRUITS JAM

GF

EF

V

Vg*

DF*

An old school classic, so easy to whip together! Silky smooth semolina pudding flavoured with vanilla and nutmeg. Top with a super-simple sugar-free jam, which will keep for up to 2 weeks in your fridge, ready to be gobbled up by your hungry little ones!

🍴 **2 adults and 2 littles**
⏱ **15 minutes**

500ml (16fl oz) full-fat
   (whole) milk or
   plant-based
   alternative*
75g (2½oz) semolina
1 tsp pure vanilla extract
1 tbsp maple syrup or
   honey* (optional,
   honey should only be
   served to babies over
   12 months)
pinch of ground nutmeg

NO-SUGAR BABY JAM
250g (9oz) frozen mixed
   summer fruit berries
2 tbsp chia seeds

Add the milk, semolina, vanilla, syrup and nutmeg to a saucepan set over a medium heat. Whisk all the ingredients together until well combined, then lower the heat and let it simmer for 12–15 minutes until thickened. Whisk often to help it thicken and to stop the pudding sticking to the bottom of the pan.

Meanwhile, make the jam by adding the berries and chia seeds to a small saucepan with 75ml (2½fl oz) water. Let it simmer for 8–10 minutes until thickened. Halfway through cooking, use a potato masher to mash the fruit, which makes it more baby friendly in texture, and helps to thicken the consistency. After 10 minutes, transfer to a glass bowl. The jam will be quite runny straight out of the pan, but will start to thicken as it cools. It'll keep in the fridge for up to 2 weeks and is great served on toast, in porridge or in pastries.

Once the semolina is thick, serve with a good dollop of jam on top. You can add some more cold milk to the pudding to loosen the consistency if you desire.

Any leftover semolina pudding can be kept in the fridge for up to 3 days, or freeze in portions for up to 3 months. Pop in a saucepan or microwave from frozen, with an extra splash of milk, and cook until piping hot inside.

SMOOTH VANILLA RICE PUDDING WITH CINNAMON APPLES

Creamy and comforting, a classic family recipe with the addition of glorious festive cinnamon apples. A delicious way to increase your family's calcium intake.

🍴 2 adults and 2 littles

⏱ 25 minutes

250ml (9fl oz) full-fat (whole) milk or plant-based alternative*

100g (3½oz) short-grain pudding rice

2 tsp pure vanilla extract

CINNAMON APPLES

2 Gala eating apples

20g (½oz) unsalted butter or dairy free spread*

2 tsp honey or maple syrup* (optional, honey should only be served to babies over 12 months)

1 tsp ground cinnamon

Add the milk, rice and vanilla to a saucepan and bring to the boil, then lower the heat and simmer for 25 minutes. Be careful the pan doesn't over-boil, as milk has a tendency to froth up quickly and spill over your hob (stovetop). Keep the heat to a minimum, and place a wooden spoon over the top of the pan to try and avoid this happening.

Stir often and cook until the rice is soft with no firm texture or bite when tasted. You may need to keep topping up with more milk if you feel the rice isn't cooked yet, but all the liquid has been soaked up.

Meanwhile, peel and core the apples, and chop into 1cm (½in) chunks. Heat a frying pan with the butter, then add the apples, honey or maple syrup and the ground cinnamon, and stir well to coat the apples in the cinnamon butter. Lower the heat and cook for 10–15 minutes, stirring every so often, until the apples have cooked down and are super soft.

Once the rice pudding is cooked, it's ready to serve with a scattering of the delicious cinnamon apples on top.

If you want to make the rice pudding super smooth for baby, take half the amount of pudding, 2 tbsp of the cinnamon apples and an extra 3 tbsp of cold milk, and blend using a hand-held blender or food processor until smooth and creamy. Add more milk if needed. You can also just whizz up the rice pudding, and mash the cinnamon apples on the side with the back of a fork and serve on top of the smooth rice pudding.

This rice pudding will keep in the fridge for 3 days, or freezer for 3 months. Defrost thoroughly and reheat in a saucepan with an extra splash of milk.

SWEET SPICED COUSCOUS PUDDING

Couscous is such an underrated kitchen store cupboard ingredient; so quick to cook and a fantastic carrier for a variety of flavours. Try this sweet couscous variation, flavoured with comforting vanilla, mixed spice and sweet banana, and bejewelled with plump, juicy raisins.

🍴 2 adults and 2 littles

⏱ 15 minutes

50g (1¾oz) (dark) raisins (optional)

1 banana, mashed

130g (4½oz) dried couscous

1 tsp pure vanilla extract

1 tsp mixed spice

400ml (14fl oz) unsweetened soya (soy) or full-fat (whole) milk*

Place the raisins, if using, on a chopping board, and briefly rock a sharp knife over them to cut each one in half.

Now add all the ingredients to a saucepan and place over a medium–high heat. Cook for 10–12 minutes, stirring often until the couscous has plumped up and the pudding has thickened well. Don't leave this pudding unattended on the hob in case the milk boils over. Place a wooden spoon over the side of the saucepan to help prevent this happening, and reduce the heat if the milk is bubbling up too high in the pan.

Once cooked, allow to cool a little and serve.

Cold pudding will last in the fridge for 3 days, or freeze for up to 3 months. Defrost thoroughly and reheat in a saucepan with an extra splash of milk to help loosen the consistency. You can also blast in the microwave for a couple of minutes, stirring halfway through. Ensure the pudding is piping hot before cooling and serving.

GINGERBREAD BISCUIT ADVENT CALENDAR

Get the kids involved making this beautiful biscuit advent calendar to share as a family throughout December. Suitable for babies from 10 months.

EF

V

Vg*

DF*

🍴 24 biscuits

⏱ 20 minutes, plus chilling

5 tbsp golden (light corn) syrup (or use dark agave syrup, which has slightly less sugar content)

110g (4oz) unrefined soft brown sugar (light or dark)

150g (5½oz) unsalted butter or coconut oil*

350g (12oz) plain (all-purpose) flour

½ tsp bicarbonate of soda (baking soda)

4 tsp ground ginger

1 tsp mixed spice

2 tsp ground cinnamon

ICING

150g (5½oz) icing (confectioners') sugar

Heat the syrup, sugar and butter in a saucepan for 2–3 minutes until bubbling and melted. Allow to cool for 5 minutes.

To a large mixing bowl, add the flour, bicarbonate of soda and spices. Stir well, then make a well in the centre and pour in the syrup. Use a wooden spoon to stir until a dough is formed. Wrap in cling film (plastic wrap) and put in the fridge for at least 30 minutes, or freezer for 15 minutes to cool and firm up.

Preheat the oven to 180°C fan (200°C/400°F/Gas 6).

Take the dough out of the fridge or freezer and use straight away. If you have left it overnight, remove the dough at least 1 hour before use to soften up enough for rolling. Cut it into quarters. Knead it a little in your hands then press into a rough circle. Roll to around 5mm (¼in) in thickness. Use Christmas cookie cutters to make 24 biscuits. Smaller biscuits keep for longer without going soft, especially if you wish to hang them. If you plan to hang the biscuits, use a chopstick to pierce a hole at the top of each cookie to thread string through once baked.

Place each biscuit on a non-stick baking tray leaving at least 2cm (¾in) between each one, and bake for 10–12 minutes until just starting to go dark brown around the edges. They will still feel very soft when coming out of the oven, however they will quickly harden as they cool. Transfer to a wire rack to cool completely.

Sift the icing sugar into a bowl, then trickle cold water into the sugar, and keep stirring until you have a loose but firm mixture. Put the icing into a food storage or disposable piping (pastry) bag and cut the end of the piping bag point, no more than 2mm (¹⁄₁₆in) from the edge; this will give you nice neat writing.

Number your biscuits from 1 to 24, and add any decoration you desire. This part is great to get the kids involved. Allow the icing to set before either packing the biscuits into a lovely festive tin, or threading with string and hanging on a foraged branch.

CELEBRATION CAKE

V

Celebrate birthdays, Easter, Mother's or Father's Day, or even just a Sunday family gathering with this low-sugar, super-light sponge cake. A total crowd-pleaser!

🍴 **8–10 adults and littles**

⏲ **30 minutes**

160g (5¾oz) unsalted butter
90g (3oz) golden caster (superfine) sugar
5 large (US extra-large) eggs
2 tsp pure vanilla extract
90g (3oz) shop-bought 100% apple purée (use a baby food pouch)
200g (7oz) self-raising (self-rising) flour
1½ tsp baking powder

FILLING

75g (2½oz) thick full-fat Greek-style yogurt
2 tsp pure vanilla extract
35g (1oz) icing (confectioners') sugar
100g (3½oz) honey or maple syrup (optional, honey should only be served to babies over 12 months)
300ml (10fl oz) double (heavy) cream
300g (10oz) strawberries
100g (3½oz) raspberries
100g (3½oz) blueberries
2 x 20cm (8in) cake tins, greased and base-lined with non-stick baking paper

Preheat the oven to 180°C fan (200°C/400°F/Gas 6). Melt the butter and set it aside to cool.

Add the caster sugar and eggs to a large bowl, and whisk on high using an electric whisk or stand mixer for 3–5 minutes until the mixture has doubled or tripled in size, and is pale and frothy.

Quickly add the vanilla extract, cooled melted butter and apple purée, then whisk again straight away on high for 30 seconds.

Sift the flour and baking powder into the wet mixture in 4 stages. Use a spatula to very gently fold the first lot of flour into the eggs, quickly and confidently, but don't lose all the air you have added to the batter. Stop mixing as soon as you see no loose dry flour, then sift in a little more and repeat.

Divide between the two cake tins, level the tops and place on the same shelf in the oven for 20–25 minutes until a knife or skewer comes out clean. Do not open the door before 20 minutes as this will cause the cakes to sink.

Allow to sit in the tins for 10 minutes, before running a knife around the edge of each sponge, then turning out onto a wire rack. If you can, peel away the baking paper as this will help the cake cool more quickly.

For the filling, add the yogurt, vanilla, icing sugar and honey or syrup to a large bowl. Whisk until creamy and combined, then add the cream. Whisk using an electric whisk for a minute or so until you have a thick cream that holds its shape. Be careful not to over-whisk as this will cause the cream to separate.

Cut the tops off the strawberries, and slice half of them thinly. To assemble the cake, lay one sponge on your serving plate. Spread half the cream evenly up to the edges. Top with the sliced strawberries and half the blueberries and raspberries. Top with the second sponge and repeat. Halve the remaining strawberries and scatter over the top of the cake with the remaining fruit.

Resources

A NOTE ABOUT PORTION SIZES

As adults, we have recommended portion sizes, as a guide to ensure we don't over-eat and essentially put on extra weight. However, for babies, there are no recommended portion sizes. Every baby is different – they learn to eat at a different pace and have different activity levels and appetites. Be mindful of your baby's wet and dirty nappies, ensure they are steadily putting on weight and, if you have any concerns, contact your health visitor or doctor.

Remember, before the age of one, food is all about exploring different tastes and textures as well as adding additional vital nutrients to baby's diet. Milk is still baby's main source of nutrition. So with that knowledge in mind, parents can relax from the worry that baby hasn't eaten enough. Focus on encouraging baby to try a variety of foods. If baby just picks it up and takes one mouthful, that's totally fine! Equally if baby wolfs down the whole lot that is fine too – they may be going through a growth spurt and need these extra calories.

The great thing about taking a baby-led weaning approach, is that it encourages baby to follow their own appetite. Baby is more likely to be able to recognize when they are full and stop eating – or start playing with the food!

DOES MY BABY NEED SNACKS?

As baby starts to drop their daytime milk feeds around the age of 8–9 months, you may want to replace this milk feed with a small snack. However, not all babies need this snack. If you are noticing that baby quite happily grazes on food through the day but struggles to sit down for a full meal, then it may be worth removing snacks to see if it gives them more of an appetite for their meals.

Equally, if baby eats well at mealtimes but is also showing signs that they need a top up mid-morning or afternoon, there is nothing wrong with offering this. All babies eat different amounts so try not to compare.

EATING ENVIRONMENTS

I feel like a broken record, but... eating together is SO important! It allows your child to learn from your healthy eating habits to teach them how it's done.

Mealtimes can be a lovely time to spend together as a family, however it can also feel challenging when little one refuses to eat their food. Try and create a consistent happy environment so your child looks forward to mealtimes.

- Get some music on – something nice and relaxing that you can sing along to or have a little jig in your seats.
- Smile lots – sounds obvious, but if your little one sees you enjoying mealtimes, they are more likely to have a good time too. And a happy baby is more likely to eat.
- Try to be consistent with where your child eats at home. If possible, eat together at a table and leave eating on the sofa to treat times.
- Eat meals at the same time every day (within reason) so your little ones can get into a good eating routine.
- Turn off the TV and put away distracting toys, which your baby will want to play with instead of eating.
- Talk lots – ask your little one to name what's on their plate or if they are young, point to what they have and say what the food is called. Then take a bite of the food from your plate, making lots of yummy noises as you do so.
- If your little messy monster makes a spillage or drops food, as frustrating as it is, try not to show stress whilst you clean it up. Get baby to help you so they understand the process.
- Food throwing is really common and can last up to around 18 months of age. There is no real way to stop your baby from throwing food; it's a developmental phase. I always made a point to never give my Nina the food back that she threw on the floor, so she would understand that if she threw her food she wouldn't be able to eat it anymore. I didn't react in my facial expressions, but picked up the food and placed it to the side and carried on with our meal.

GETTING YOUR LITTLE ONE INVOLVED IN THE KITCHEN

Cooking with your mini chef – allowing them to be involved in mealtime decisions and learning the process of how food is prepared – can really help them to overcome fussiness.

Cooking with your child helps increase their language development through listening to and understanding your instructions. It increases their focus and attention, and helps to develop their fine motor skills. It also allows them to explore food using all of their senses (look, smell, touch) outside of mealtime!

- Invest in a sturdy stool, preferably one with sides so your child is at a safe height at the kitchen counter.
- Ensure your child never uses sharp knives or utensils. If you ask them to chop something up, ensures it's super soft so the force doesn't harm their little fingers, and use a blunt blade like a dinner knife or special children's knife.
- Put soft herbs, meat and veg in a high-sided jug (pitcher) and little ones can use a pair of scissors to chop it up instead.
- It goes without saying, keep your child away from high heat sources like the kettle, cooker or oven.
- Help your little one when it's tricky or dangerous, but also allow them some independence where possible to grow their confidence and skill level.
- Never leave your child unattended whilst they are cooking in the kitchen.

DOES YOUR LITTLE ONE OFTEN REFUSE THE FOOD YOU COOK?

Even the most adventurous little eater will go through fussy phases. It's incredibly normal, as babies grow older and gain more independence they like to test boundaries and develop their likes and dislikes. It's our job as parents to ensure that these phases don't become the norm.

Did your baby eat everything in the first 6 months of weaning, and then suddenly between 12–18 months they started to refuse foods which once would have been gobbled up? Don't blame yourself. Your baby is growing and gaining independence, fine-tuning their awareness of their own appetite and therefore less likely to eat if they really don't want to.

Some research suggests that the reason toddlers become fussy stems from their primeval survival mechanism, preventing mobile toddlers from eating everything in sight, which could have been poisonous and dangerous.

There are many reasons as to why babies and toddlers decide to refuse their meal: they aren't hungry enough; they're too tired and irritable; they're distracted by the TV or toys; or something about the texture is putting them off (this doesn't mean they won't like it the next time you offer it). It's rarely because your child genuinely does not like the taste of a certain food. The trick is to keep offering it, baby will come round.

When your little one begins their fussy phase, try not to worry that they aren't "getting enough" or "they will be hungry" and therefore offering an alternative food when the original meal is refused. Baby will remember this action and you will find that fussiness will persist.

By eating together you can show baby how exciting it is to explore a variety of flavours. Offer new foods to your family often, so eating new flavours becomes the norm and they are less likely to refuse when faced with an unfamiliar ingredient. Try not to always offer something you "know" they will like, as unintentionally you will be limiting their diet and stopping them overcoming this fussy phase.

If your little one says they don't like the meal and stops eating, it's important that you carry on dining to show your child how much you are enjoying the food. Don't put any pressure on them to carry on eating, but do insist that they need to stay seated at the table until everyone has finished eating. You may find that they will start to eat as they watch everyone enjoying the food.

Keep offering new foods. It can feel like you are making the food to be wasted, but fussy children won't get over their fear of trying a new food if they aren't exposed to it. It can take up to 10 times of offering a new food for your little one to like it, or even try it. Tastes change as they grow older too, so hang in there and keep offering on a regular basis.

TAKE THE PRESSURE OFF
If they don't eat, it's okay! You may find the less pressure your little one has, the more likely they will dig in.

HOW TO INTRODUCE ALLERGENIC FOODS

Offering allergenic foods to baby for the first time can be a worry for parents. However, if there is no history of atopic (allergic) disease, including eczema, asthma and hayfever, in the family, then the risk is low for a serious reaction. With that being said, it's best to go sensibly and cautiously. But don't be tempted to avoid them altogether. There is no evidence to support delaying introduction to these foods after 6 months.

Serve the following common food allergens to baby initially as a single flavour in small amounts. Offer first thing in the morning so you can monitor baby for any reactions throughout the day. If you do not detect a reaction, continue to offer these foods multiple times a week as part of a varied diet. Try to leave a gap of three days between introduction of each new allergenic food to monitor for signs of reaction.

COMMON FOOD ALLERGENS

- Cow's milk
- Egg
- Foods containing gluten, including rye, wheat, barley
- Nuts and peanuts (serve crushed, ground or as a nut butter)
- Sesame seeds
- Soya
- Mustard
- Celery
- Molluscs
- Fish
- Shellfish (don't serve raw or lightly cooked)

COMMON ALLERGIC REACTIONS

- Diarrhoea or vomiting
- A cough
- Wheezing and shortness of breath
- Itchy throat and tongue
- Itchy skin or rash
- Swollen lips and throat
- Runny or blocked nose
- Sore, red and itchy eyes

If you think your child is having an allergic reaction, seek medical advice. For babies considered at higher risk of food allergy, including those who already have a diagnosed food allergy or eczema, which developed early in life and/or is persistent or problematic, it may be beneficial to speak with GP about seeing a specialist for advice.

WHAT YOU NEED TO KNOW ABOUT MILK!

0–12 MONTHS

- For around the first 6 months of baby's life, you should exclusively feed them on breast milk or first-infant formula. Their little tummies are not yet mature and developed enough to be able to process more complex foods.
- Unless you have been medically advised otherwise, cow's or goat's milk first-infant formula is the only alternative to breast milk in the first 12 months of life.
- Cow's milk or plant-based alternatives are safe to offer baby as an ingredient in a meal (mixed in with solid foods), raw or cooked, from the age of 6 months.
- Do not replace baby's usual breast or formula feed with alternative milks before the age of 12 months, as they do not contain the same level of nutrients.
- From the age of 12 months, you can offer your toddler cow's milk or calcium-fortified plant-based alternative to replace breast or formula feeds, if you want.

GOOD TO NOTE

- Avoid offering rice drinks to children under 5; they contain high levels of arsenic.
- Semi-skimmed milk should be avoided for children under 2, as they need high levels of fat in their food to ensure sufficient calorie intake. (This applies to other dairy products, too, always offer full-fat versions.)
- Avoid serving skimmed milk to children under 5; it doesn't contain enough calories.
- If you are using a plant-based milk alternative, ensure it is fortified with key nutrients like calcium, and aim for a options providing similar amounts of energy (calories) and (where possible) protein provided by full-fat cow's milk.

HOW WILL YOUR BABY'S MILK INTAKE CHANGE DURING WEANING?

The simple answer is, to start with, nothing will change. When your baby first starts weaning, the amount of solid foods they consume will be very small. They will still get the majority of their nutrients from their milk.

Offer baby their milk at the same time of day as before you started weaning, and try to slot in solid foods in between milk feeds. As you gradually increase the number of meals baby is having a day, you may notice a decrease in their interest in daytime feeds. This is a good time to try to remove one or two of baby's milk feeds in between breakfast and lunch, or dinner.

This usually happens between the age of 7–10 months, however, all babies are different and have varied levels of appetite. The key is to follow baby's lead and let them tell you when they are ready. A general aim is for baby to be eating only solid food meals through the day by the time they are 12 months of age (with bedtime and night time feeds still in place). However, this is a general rule and every baby is different. Breastfed babies in particular may be feeding more than this, which is completely normal.

If you find that weaning baby onto solid food is going a little slowly, by the time your little one is 10–11 months, and baby is much preferring milk to solid food, you could try decreasing the quantity or frequency of milk offered, and replace it with a snack to encourage baby along.

MEAL PLANNER

Spoilt for choice and not sure what to cook next week? Here's an example family meal plan that is suitable when your baby is eating 3 meals a day. Not every baby will need snacks, so feel free to remove to suit your child's appetite. Sundays are family days for us and I often take the time off from routine.

	Breakfast	Snack	Lunch	Snack	Dinner
Monday	Carrot Cake Porridge, see page 107	Halved blueberries and sliced or grated cheese	3-Minute Pasta Sauce, see page 46	Peanut Butter Soft-bake Cookies, see page 164	My First Curry, see page 88
Tuesday	Baby porridge fingers, see page 20, with yogurt	Rice cake with nut butter	Cheesy broccoli orzo, see page 59	Carrot and apple soft oaty bars, see page 165	Spinach and ricotta puff parcels, see page 102
Wednesday	1, 2, 3 pancakes, see page 38, with yogurt	Chia cheese crackers, see page 176	Cheat's beef ragu, see page 71	Bowl of steamed broccoli	One-pan lemon salmon with courgette and potato wedges, see page 72
Thursday	Bacon, cheese and chive muffins, see page 36, with fresh fruit	Fruit salad and lime yogurt dip, see page 171	Carrot, chive and cheese toastie, see page 55	Hummus and cucumber and breadsticks, see page 45	Lasagne roll-ups, see page 120
Friday	Berry cheesecake bowl with toasted oat crumb, see page 34	Half a piece of toast with cream cheese and berries	Chicken noodle soup, see page 56	Carrot cake baby bliss ball, see page 174	Gorgeous grains cheat's risotto, see page 83
Saturday	Mexican baked eggs, see page 24	Almond and prune muffins, see page 173	Spinach and sweetcorn muffins, see page 108	Chia cheese crackers, see page 176	Cheesy arancini balls, see page 84

THROW-TOGETHER PLATES

Sometimes we want to feed the family quickly and easily by raiding the cupboards and fridge to serve up a picky selection of food that's well-balanced but super-easy to prep. These are also great for packed lunches and snacks in smaller portions.

PLATE 1
Sliced cheese
Unsalted rice cake with nut butter
Steamed broccoli
Strawberries

PLATE 2
Hummus, see page 45
Breadsticks
Cucumber sticks
Halved blueberries

PLATE 3
Crackers
Sliced cheese
Cooked meat
Grated carrot
Cucumber chunks

PLATE 4
Hard-boiled egg
Toast
Leftovers from your freezer stash, like the fritters pictured here
Avocado fingers

STORAGE AND FREEZING GUIDELINES

Storing and freezing food safely is important, especially when feeding little tummies. Check the table on pages 212-213 for specific ingredients.

HOW TO STORE FOOD IN THE FRIDGE
- Store leftovers in airtight containers in the fridge. This not only slows down the growth of bacteria, but helps to stop other food flavours leaching into it.
- Fully cool food before putting it in the fridge.
- Cool food as quickly as possible (within 2 hours) by spreading it evenly on a cool surface. If you are storing rice, ensure it is fully cooled and refrigerated within 1 hour of cooking.
- Most cooked food will last for 2 days in the fridge, however some more perishable foods (such as cooked fish) will last for only 24 hours.
- Always store raw meat on a separate shelf from fresh fruit and vegetables.

HOW TO STORE FOOD IN THE FREEZER
- Package up all foods in airtight containers or bags to prevent freezer burn.
- Freeze in portions, so you only need to defrost what you need.
- To freeze things like fritters, place a small square of baking paper in between each item to stop them sticking together.
- Label and date the food you put in the freezer.
- Never freeze meat or fish twice.
- You can defrost fruit and veg, cook with them, then freeze that cooked meal.
- Always store raw frozen meat on a different shelf to frozen fruit and veg, as this may be eaten uncooked.

REHEATING FOOD FROM THE FRIDGE OR FREEZER
- Some food, such as fritters, can be eaten cold after storing in the fridge or defrosting, as long as it was fully cooked beforehand (with the exception of fruit like berries, which can be eaten uncooked after defrosting).
- When reheating food, ensure it is piping hot before cooling and serving to kill any bacteria.
- Fully defrost frozen food in the fridge before reheating and serving, unless it can be cooked from frozen.
- If you defrost food at room temperature, keep an eye on it and place in the fridge as soon as it is defrosted.
- Foods that are raw inside need to be defrosted first, as when cooking the outside will cook and burn before the inside has had a chance to cook. However foods like fritters can be reheated in the microwave from frozen until piping hot.
- Leftovers should only ever be reheated once and consumed within 24 hours.

Food	How to store in the fridge	Freezing instructions	Defrosting/reheating instructions
Yogurt	Keep covered in the fridge and use by the use by date.	Can be frozen for up to 3 months, but best avoided as it can separate on defrosting.	Frozen yogurt is best served still frozen like an ice cream. Thawed yogurt will separate – it will still be okay to eat, but the texture will be very different.
Cooked fish	Cool, tightly cover and store in the fridge for 24 hours. Eat cold, or reheat until piping hot in the oven or microwave.	As long as the fish was not frozen prior to cooking, leftover cooked fish can be frozen for up to 1 month.	Place in the fridge overnight to thaw, and reheat until piping hot in the oven or microwave.
Fruit	Soft perishable fruit like berries are best kept in the fridge. All others are fine to keep in the fruit bowl. TIP: *If you would like fruit to ripen quicker, store in the same bowl as a banana.*	Fruits and veg will last in the freezer for 12 months. *(Most fruit, particularly bananas, will benefit from peeling, chopping and storing in an airtight container before freezing.)*	Frozen fruit can be cooked from frozen, or allow to thaw at room temperature and eat cold. Frozen fruit also blends well to make instant healthy ice cream (see page 179).
Rice	Cool cooked rice within an hour by spreading it thinly on a plate, then quickly transfer to an airtight container. Store in the fridge for up to 24 hours. When reheating, ensure it is piping hot.	Cool quickly (within an hour) and freeze for up to 1 month.	You can defrost rice in the fridge and reheat until piping hot in the microwave, or you can reheat straight from frozen but ensure it is piping hot. Do not reheat rice more than once.

Food	How to store in the fridge	Freezing instructions	Defrosting/reheating instructions
Veg and fruit purée	Store in a lidded container for 48 hours in the fridge.	Store the purée in ice cube trays, small pots or ice lolly moulds, and freeze for up to 3 months.	Put into a microwaveable dish, add a splash of water and microwave for a couple of minutes until piping hot. Alternatively, defrost thoroughly and reheat in a saucepan with a splash of water.
Any baby purée containing meat, eggs or fish	Store in a lidded container for 24 hours in the fridge.	Store in ice cube trays or small pots, and freeze for up to 1 month.	Put into a microwaveable dish, add a splash of water and microwave for a couple of minutes until piping hot. Alternatively, defrost thoroughly and reheat in a saucepan with a splash of water.
Pancakes and fritters	Cover and store in the fridge for up to 3 days.	Freeze in portions (with baking paper in between each fritter to prevent sticking) for up to 3 months.	Defrost from frozen in the microwave or defrost thoroughly at room temperature, and heat in the oven until piping hot.

FOOD YOU SHOULD AVOID FREEZING

• Eggs in their shell.
• Fresh veg which has a high water content like celery, lettuce and cucumber.
• Emulsions, such as mayonnaise.
• Soft cheese and dairy products with a high water content (such as yogurt).

INGREDIENTS THAT I ALWAYS HAVE IN

These are all items I keep in my pantry and fridge for making simple and nutritious meals for my family. You may need to buy additional ingredients for specific recipes. My famous five (opposite) are things that I always have in stock!

STORE CUPBOARD

- Low-salt stock cubes (vegetable, chicken and beef)
- Worcestershire sauce
- Low-salt soy sauce
- Sunflower oil
- Garlic-infused olive oil
- Olive or coconut oil cooking spray
- Coconut oil
- Sesame oil
- Red wine vinegar
- Tomato purée (paste)
- No added sugar or salt ketchup
- Dried pasta in a variety of shapes
- Dried uncooked rice

- (basmati or long grain)
- Packets of ready-cooked mixed grains or rice (unsalted and unflavoured)
- Dried couscous
- Panko and plain breadcrumbs
- Rolled (old-fashioned) porridge oats
- Eggs (medium British Lion-stamped)
- Brown and red onions
- White potatoes
- Sweet potatoes
- Butternut squash

- Garlic bulbs
- Coconut milk (full-fat for the little ones)
- Canned tuna in spring water
- Canned sweetcorn in water (no added salt)
- Canned chopped tomatoes
- Passata (strained tomatoes)
- Variety of canned beans in water (no added salt)
- Canned chickpeas in water
- White sliced bread
- Tortilla wraps
- Crumpets

BAKING CUPBOARD

- Plain (all-purpose) flour
- Self-raising (self-rising) flour
- Cornflour (cornstarch)
- Baking powder
- Pure vanilla extract (not essence)
- Unsweetened cocoa powder

- Seedless raisins
- 100% apple purée pouches (find in the baby aisle)
- Peanut butter (100% nuts with no palm oil)
- Honey (do not serve honey to babies under 12 months)

- Maple syrup
- Ground flaxseeds (linseeds)
- Desiccated coconut (dried unsweetened shredded)
- Chia seeds (whole or ground)
- Sesame seeds

HERBS AND SPICES

- Mild garam masala
- Mild curry powder
- Garlic granules
- Smoked paprika

- Ground cumin
- Ground cinnamon
- Ground ginger
- Mixed spice

- Mixed dried herbs
- Black pepper mill

FRIDGE

- Full-fat Greek-style yogurt
- Cheddar (medium or strong strength)
- Full-fat cream cheese
- Full-fat (whole) milk
- Ready-rolled puff pastry
- Unsalted butter
- Broccoli
- Green beans
- Carrots
- Cucumber
- Courgettes (zucchini)
- Berries, such as raspberries and blueberries
- Chives

FRUIT BOWL

- Bananas
- Apples
- Satsumas
- Avocados
- Lemons
- Limes

FREEZER

- Frozen spinach cubes
- Frozen mixed veg
- Frozen broccoli
- Frozen peas
- Frozen mixed berries and fruit

1. PLAIN GREEK YOGURT

2. CHEDDAR CHEESE

5. CANNED TUNA

MY FAMOUS FIVE

3. TOMATO PURÉE

4. SELF-RAISING FLOUR

TIME-SAVING COOKING TIPS AND TRICKS

When you are looking after the little ones and trying to cook at the same time, we need to get it done as quickly as possible. Here's a few tricks and tips that help shave off a few moments here and there.

Boiling a pot of water

1. Fill the kettle up to the brim and bring up to a rolling boil.
2. Meanwhile grab your saucepan and add 1cm (½in) of tap water to the bottom of the pan. Now place this on a high heat.
3. Once the kettle is boiled, the pan should be simmering and steaming. Add the kettle water to the pan. As it's going into a warm pan, the water will be boiling within minutes and ready for adding the pasta.

To stop the pasta water boiling over

Rest a wooden spoon over the top of the pan.

When making pasta or cheese sauce

Add a ladle or so to an ice cube tray and pop in the freezer once cooled. Now you have a quick grab pasta sauce when the cupboards are looking bare.

To use up those fruits and veggies that are going past their best

Prep everyone's morning smoothie by cutting up a selection of produce and separating into portions to freeze. In the morning add the frozen fruit and veg to a blender with a splash of milk or yogurt.

Ideas to get ahead

- When making dinner, use an unused hob (stove top) ring to boil some eggs for 10 minutes, then quickly cool in a big pot of cold water. Once cooled, these will last in the fridge for up to 5 days. Perfect protein to add to your family meals or lunch boxes.
- Make a batch of sugar-free jam (see page 192) for an easy accompaniment to your family meals, which will keep for up to 2 weeks.
- Wash and dry your veggies all in one go before storing in the fridge to save time when cooking meals.

Don't have a garlic crusher?

Use a large sharp kitchen knife to roughly chop the garlic. Then place the blade on its side and use the sharp edge to press and squish the garlic to a paste. You can then rock the knife over it to cut into a very fine paste.

Or use the fine setting on your box grater to grate the cloves into a fine paste.

Eggs always crack when boiling?
Use a sharp thumb tack, push pin or buy an egg pricker to pierce a small hole at the point of each egg. This lets the air escape and stop the shell cracking.

Struggling to juice your limes or lemons?
Roll the fruit with a fair amount of pressure on the work surface to burst some of the juicy segments before cutting and juicing.

Fridge cold butter too hard to spread?
Run very hot water from the tap into a small glass to heat it up. Then place a small knob (pat) of butter onto a saucer and cover with the hot glass. After a couple of minutes the butter will be soft enough to spread.

TIPS FOR KEEPING BABY ENTERTAINED

Keeping baby entertained while you cook is a daunting task, so here are a few ideas to help save your sanity while you get on with preparing the family meal.

- Tape straws and spoons to baby's highchair with masking or washi tape. Baby will love trying to remove them. You can also simply apply tape to baby's highchair in lots of different angles, and watch while baby tries to peel them off.
- Stuff an array of multicoloured pom poms into a large whisk and let baby try to pick them out!
- If you can stand the noise: let baby bang the base of your pots and pans with a wooden spoon in the corner of the kitchen.
- Make a kitchen sensory basket. Include things like a whisk, ice cube tray, tea towel, sponge, wooden spoon, small baking tray, plastic cup and spoon.
- Head online and buy an emergency foil blanket (costs pennies) and watch as your baby has hours *minutes* of fun!
- The lovely food stylist for this book, Maud, told me she gives her twins quarter of a pomegranate and allows them to spend time picking out all of the juicy seeds. Great for babies starting to develop their pincer grip.
- Older kids love getting involved in the kitchen; ask them to peel a satsuma or mix the bowl. It may help them become more adventurous with what they eat.
- Don't feel guilty to pop the telly on for 10 minutes if that works!

WEANING ON THE GO

Eating out with baby can initially seem daunting. The mess, the stress, what to pack... so much to think about! Try not to let this put you off from spending quality time with baby out and about. It's good to get your little one used to eating in different environments; variety in food, location and company.

You can of course order from the menu, however, often variety isn't great and the kids' menu is a little unhealthy. Don't be scared to order a small plate from the adult menu, or ask the waiter if you can modify some dishes to suit your baby's diet. Try to ask for no salt to be used when cooking baby's meal where possible.

Equally, it is completely fine to bring your own food for babies and toddlers to a restaurant. The way I see it, if I'm ordering for myself its okay to bring something for my little one. I often will buy my Nina a glass of milk, essentially don't use the establishment as a canteen and it's totally fine.

ESSENTIAL PACKING LIST

1. **Toys and entertainment** for while you're waiting for your food. I find one toy, a book and a little light snack helps. Try a small tub of cooked peas, or blueberries – something that isn't going to fill baby up.
2. Baby's usual **plate**, and if its a suction plate, even better. Saves too much mess on the restaurant floor.
3. Baby's usual **cutlery** – often establishments don't have baby-friendly cutlery.
4. Baby's usual **drinking cup**.
5. A good **bib**.
6. **Muslin or wet wipes** to clean up your mucky little pup. You can also give the highchair and table around your baby a quick wipe down before eating, as often the trays aren't cleaned between each customer.

If you're packing your own food for baby, leftovers are great. If you know you're going out tomorrow, make food today that is easily transportable, such as fritters, veggie flapjacks or muffins. Or do a good freezer raid. Generally small muffins or fritters will defrost in around 4 hours, so take them out of the freezer first thing ready for your plans later that day.

INDEX

THANK YOU

I want to start by saying a massive thank you to every one of you who follows along with @whatmummymakes on Instagram. For saving, sharing, making and enjoying my recipes with your loved ones. This book wouldn't be possible without you!

To my inspiration, Nina! Before you came along, I had no idea how much I would enjoy feeding my child and watching you enjoy food as much as I do! Thank you for making every meal time a joy and bringing the biggest smile to my face.

Big thank you to my friends and family, my husband Stu. To my Mum, for raising me to love food and family meal times (even if I did protest it during those teenage years). We sat at the table every breakfast and dinner, eating an adventurous array of flavourful food and cuisines. You are the foundation for my love of food! To my dear pal Joanna, for always being there! And little Charlotte, for being my Nini's BFF! And finally, to the friends I have made on this WMM journey, you have helped me to develop my style and pushed me to always share my true self.

To all the team at DK and my fantastic editor Steph, for putting so much love and thought into this book. Sophie on design, and Kate the copy editor, you're amazing thank you! I had so much fun at the photoshoots, Hannah on props, the food team Maud and her assistants Flossie and Sophie, you're fab! Clare, our amazing photographer, thank you for bringing this book to life! Sorry for always wanting everything symmetrical!

Thank you to my agent and friend Darryl, for believing in my idea and helping to make it a reality.

I want to say a big thank you to bamboo bamboo for supplying the cutest range of sustainable bamboo baby tableware. I've been using your products since my Nina was wee; a weaning must for me! Scandiborn, thank you for injecting a bit of Scandi chic into the book, from bibs to toys – thank you for your generosity.

I must also thank our gorgeous babies who modelled in this book. Thank you Alieze, Antonia, Arthur, Ben, Felix, Oscar, Rayaan and, of course, my Nina.

And last but certainly not least I want to give an incredibly big THANK YOU to our National Health Service! All of my weaning advice in this book is based on NHS guidelines, backed up by our fantastic nutritionist Lucy Upton whom is also an NHS paediatric dietitian.

I hope you have all enjoyed this book, I can't wait to see your cook-ups!

Penguin
Random
House

Photographer Clare Winfield
Food stylist Maud Eden
Prop stylist Hannah Wilkinson
Make-up artist Madge Foster
Indexer Hilary Bird
Editor Kate Reeves-Brown
Nutritionist Lucy Upton
Designer Sophie Yamamoto
Jacket Designer Amy Cox
Jacket Coordinator Lucy Philpott
Production Designer Vanessa Hamilton
Creative Technical Support Sonia Charbonnier
Senior Production Editor Tony Phipps
Senior Production Controller Stephanie McConnell
Managing Art Editor Christine Keilty
Senior Acquisitions Editor Stephanie Milner
Art Director Maxine Pedliham
Publishing Director Mary-Clare Jerram

First published in Great Britain in 2020 by
Dorling Kindersley Limited
One Embassy Gardens, 8 Viaduct Gardens,
London, SW11 7BW

Text copyright © 2020 Rebecca Wilson
Copyright © 2020 Dorling Kindersley Limited
A Penguin Random House Company
13
017–320736–Jul/2020

A CIP catalogue record for this book
is available from the British Library.
ISBN: 978-0-2414-5515-9
Printed in Scotland

For the curious

www.dk.com

MIX
Paper from
responsible sources
FSC™ C018179

PLEASE NOTE
• All eggs are medium (UK) or large (US) unless otherwise specified. Uncooked or partially cooked eggs should not be served to those with compromised immune systems.
• Those following strict allergen diets should always check the packet for guidance about suitability.
• Soy sauce is normally very high in salt and not recommended for use in baby or toddlers foods for this reason. Choosing a lower salt soy sauce can be therefore be a good swap for the whole family – but be careful each brand is different with some still containing too much salt. Try to chose a low salt variety that has less than 6g/100mls of salt on the label

STILL HUNGRY?
Follow @whatmummymakes
for much more.